Fintan O'Toole is an acclaimed historian, biographer and critic. As a columnist with the *Irish Times*, he is Ireland's most respected and controversial political commentator, whose name was almost a term of abuse among the politicians who presided over the economic debacle of recent years. His books include *White Savage* (Faber and Faber) and *A Traitor's Kiss*.

D0109064

by the same author

SHAKESPEARE IS HARD, BUT SO IS LIFE
A TRAITOR'S KISS
WHITE SAVAGE

Ship of Fools

How Stupidity and Corruption
Sank the Celtic Tiger

FINTAN O'TOOLE

faber and faber

First published in 2009
by Faber and Faber Ltd
Bloomsbury House
74–77 Great Russell Street
London WC1B 3DA
This paperback edition first published in 2010

Typeset by Faber and Faber Ltd
Printed in England by CPI BookMarque, Croydon

A CIP record for this book
is available from the British Library

ISBN 978-0-571-26075-1

2 4 6 8 10 9 7 5 3 1

To JOHN O'REILLY and JOHN CONNOLE,
better builders

Contents

Acknowledgements

I would like to thank Dr Jim Stewart and Professor Justin O'Brien for help and advice with parts of this work, though neither of them is responsible for my use of those gifts. I am also grateful to Geraldine Kennedy, editor of the *Irish Times*, and her predecessor Conor Brady, for allowing me to express many of the ideas that are developed here, even when they were badly out of kilter with the mood of the times. Paddy Smyth and later Peter Murtagh on the opinion pages have been particularly patient and supportive.

This book would not have been undertaken without Neil Belton's support and perhaps misplaced optimism, and would not have been possible without Charles Boyle's acute work on the text. I am also grateful for the work of my agent Derek Johns.

My debt to Clare Connell is, as always, both incalculable and inexpressible.

A Note on Sources

Since this book is intended as a polemical, rather than a historical or academic work, it does not have an apparatus of references and footnotes. All of the facts and statistics used here are, however, easily available online from the relevant government departments, the Revenue Commissioners, the Comptroller and Auditor General, the Central Statistics Office, the reports and transcripts of the McCracken, Flood and Moriarty tribunals, the DIRT inquiry, the reports of the all-party Oireachtas Committee on the Constitution, the National Competitiveness Council, Eurostat, the OECD and the International Monetary Fund. References to contemporary events are drawn from the archives of the *Irish Times*, *Sunday Tribune*, *Sunday Business Post*, *Irish Independent*, *Sunday Independent* and the *Irish Mail on Sunday*.

Glossary

Dáil – the lower house of the Irish parliament

Fianna Fáil – the dominant party in Irish politics since 1932

Fine Gael – the largest opposition party

IFSRA – the Irish Financial Regulatory Authority, established in 2003 as the separate supervisory arm of the Central Bank; it was subsequently known as The Financial Regulator

Progressive Democrats – a small but highly influential neo-liberal party formed in 1985 and wound up in 2009

Protestant Ascendancy – the governing and landowning class, adhering to to the Protestant state church, that dominated Irish society from the seventeenth to the nineteenth century

Tánaiste – the deputy prime minister

Taoiseach – the prime minister

TD – member of the lower house of the Irish parliament, Dáil Éireann

Three Ships

I

In July 2004, the property developer Seán Dunne celebrated his second marriage, to the former gossip columnist Gayle Killilea, in a seventeenth-century villa on the Italian Riviera. The guests, as Ms Killilea's newspaper gushed, were 'a fascinating sample of Irish society: bankers and footballers, designers and theatre directors, not to mention, given the groom's background, political deal-makers'. The only notable absentees were the serving Taoiseach, Bertie Ahern, and his Minister for Finance, Charlie McCreevy.

Ahern had been due to arrive for the wedding, flying straight from the National Day of Commemoration ceremonies to honour Ireland's war dead, and to stay as a guest of the property magnate at the Hotel Splendido in Portofino. When news of his plans to travel to Italy was leaked to the press, he decided not to go. During the speeches, however, a phone call from Ahern was played on speakers to the guests: 'Dunner, you and I go back a long way. I wish I could be there,' he said. 'I'm sorry I couldn't come but I would have been more trouble to you than I'd be worth.' The Taoiseach, Killilea explained to the *Sunday Independent*, 'didn't want our wedding to turn into all being about him. Then Charlie McCreevy said he better not come either.'

The party cost € 1.5 million, but it was merely the prelude

to a longer, more lavish nuptial celebration. The couple had hired Aristotle Onassis's old yacht, the *Christina O*, venue for the wedding receptions of Onassis and Jackie Kennedy in 1968 and of Grace Kelly and Prince Rainier in 1956. Forty-four guests were taken on a two-week cruise around the Mediterranean. The cost of chartering the yacht is €65,000 a day, not including food, drink and fuel. The fuel charge was €575 an hour.

But the real cost of the *Christina O* was borne by a couple of million people in Ireland, who probably did not know that they had paid for much of it. The Christina O Partnership Limited is registered in the Cook Islands but owned by a consortium of Irish businessmen, who purchased it in 2000. It cost them €65 million to buy and refit the yacht in lavish style, including a bronze-bordered swimming pool inlaid with mosaic frescos of ancient Crete that, at the push of a button, could be turned into a dance floor.

The expense was largely borne by the Irish taxpayer. Under Ireland's beneficent tax regime for the rich, the wealthy businessmen who put up the cash got most of it back from the state. In November 2008, the Revenue failed in a court case in which it had challenged the right of one of the investors, Pino Harris, to claim back most of his outlay on the *Christina O*. Harris had put up €14.3 million and got €9.12 million of it from the state in the form of tax refunds. Assuming that the other investors got back the same proportion of their investment from the tax authorities, the Irish taxpayer lavished about €40 million on the *Christina O*. It was money well spent – a state in the throes of a demented property cult needed somewhere suitable for its new aristocracy to disport itself in style.

Less than a year after his epic epithalamion in the Mediterranean, Seán Dunne pushed Irish property prices to new heights by buying the Jurys and Berkeley Court hotels in Ballsbridge, Dublin, for €260 million, with the intention of demolishing them to build a new high-rise city quarter to rival London's Knightsbridge. He paid €53.7 million per acre for the land; the previous record was €35 million. He then bought a small adjacent site, Hume House, for the equivalent of €195 million an acre – believed to be one of the highest prices paid for a piece of real estate ever, anywhere. In all, he spent €379 million on his Ballsbridge site.

In August 2009, Ulster Bank, a subsidiary of the Royal Bank of Scotland, moved loans it had given Dunne to buy the Jurys and Berkeley Court site into a new 'quarantine' division for dodgy assets, a prelude to eventually offloading them to a British or Irish state 'bad bank' for toxic debts that were unlikely ever to be repaid in full.

The *Christina O* sailed on.

2

At two o'clock on the morning of 11 September 2008, twelve miles west of the island of Belle-Ile in the Bay of Biscay, the bilge alarm sounded on the Irish national yacht, the *Asgard II*. The brigantine was the successor to and namesake of the original *Asgard*, on which, in 1916, the nationalist revolutionary Erskine Childers and his wife Mary ran a consignment of German guns into Howth harbour and delivered them to the Irish Volunteers. The original ship was enshrined in nationalist mythology and eventually preserved in the national museum. The *Asgard II*, the state's official sail training vessel, inherited some of its aura as a symbol of the nation. Its masthead was an image of the sixteenth-century 'pirate queen' Granuaile, who had defied Elizabethan encroachment on her West of Ireland coastal fastness.

The sound of the alarm that morning meant that the *Asgard II* was taking in water. The captain gave the order to abandon ship, the crew was evacuated, and the *Asgard*, her decks awash, sank sadly to the bottom of the bay. There was some hope that she might be raised, but in February 2009 the government decided that there was not much hope of salvage. Nor was there much prospect of building a new boat to symbolise the nation. The government was so broke that it quietly pocketed the €3.8 million in insurance money and left the *Asgard* to its watery fate.

There was something almost too neat about the symbolism. A fortnight later, the Irish banking system, awash with waves of bad debts owed by property developers, collapsed. The great Irish economic miracle of the 1990s and early twenty-first century was over and the global Cinderella was returning to rags and ashes. The *Asgard* had never functioned quite so eloquently as an image of Ireland.

3

A joke:
A magician gets a job on a cruise ship. The captain keeps a talking parrot to amuse himself and his passengers. At first, the magician is charmed by the parrot's smart-arse repartee. When he gives his show, however, the parrot hangs out of a light fitting above his head. When the magician makes a dove disappear, the parrot squawks: 'It's up his sleeve.' When he makes a playing card vanish,

the parrot shrieks: 'It's behind his ear.' When he makes a rabbit evaporate into thin air, the bird screeches: 'It's in his hat.'

The enraged magician can't take any more and he starts to swipe at the bird with his cane. Just then the ship hits an iceberg. The magician is nearly trampled in the rush for safety and he has to dive into the water and swim. As he finally drags himself into the lifeboat, the parrot, perched on the stern, looks him in the eye and says, 'Okay, you've got me. How did you make the ship disappear?'

1

El Tigre Celta

'un "american dream" à l'européenne'
– *Le Monde* on Ireland

In Tegucigalpa, at 7 p.m. on the evening of 19 February 2009, members of the Honduran National Business Council filed into the 700-seater La Concordia ballroom of the Marriott Hotel. They had paid $150 a head to hear a lecture about the Irish economic miracle and how it could be emulated by those still wallowing in the swamps of underdevelopment. Its title was *El Tigre Celta: Modelo Irlandes de Desarrollo* ('The Celtic Tiger: The Irish Model of Development'). The speaker was the former Taoiseach, Bertie Ahern, described in the promotional literature for the event as the 'driver of the Irish economic model'.

The speech so impressed the right-wing Honduran National Party that it quickly issued a statement proclaiming its close affinity with Ahern's inspiring leadership: 'The development model followed by Ireland to become the "Celtic Tiger" coincides with that promoted by the Nationalist candidate Porfirio Lobo Sosa, nationalist leaders said after meeting with former prime minister of that European country, Bertie Ahern . . . The nationalist leadership knew all about the development programs implemented by Ahern when he served in office between 1997 and 2008 which allowed him to place Ireland at the head of the wealthiest nations of Europe at present.'

It was perhaps as well that, for most Hondurans, Ireland is a faraway country of which they know nothing. Back home, on the day after Ahern's speech about the Irish model of development, it was disclosed that the newly nationalised Anglo Irish Bank had over the previous few years given €225 million in loans to its own directors, chief among them its chairman, and Ahern's good friend, Seán FitzPatrick.

During the same week, it emerged that Anglo Irish had lent a secret consortium of investors €300 million to buy the bank's own shares. The European Commission in Brussels publicly rebuked the Irish government for failing to control the public finances during the boom years. Social welfare officials were warning that they couldn't cope with the wave of claims from the newly unemployed. A hotel in Limerick had to stop advertising staff vacancies after 2,500 people applied for 120 jobs. Ahern's highway to development was looking increasingly like a road to nowhere.

Ahern's speech on 'the Irish model of development' had been greatly in demand, not because he had any oratorical skills, but because the globalised Irish economy had itself become a global brand. He had delivered the same script in both Korea and Ecuador in October 2008 – reportedly for a fee of €30,000 each time.

Sadly, this source of income dried up as news of the collapse of the Irish economy finally reached distant parts. In early August 2009, the Celtic Tiger speech was quietly dropped from Ahern's portfolio by his agents, the Washington Speakers Bureau. The Irish model of development had come to seem more like a threat than a promise.

By then, Ireland was outstanding in the global economy, but not quite in the way that Ahern's listeners might have been told about. The International Monetary Fund was predicting that Ireland's Gross Domestic Product (GDP) would shrink by 13.5 per cent in 2009 and 2010 – the worst performance among all the advanced economies and one of the worst ever recorded in peacetime in the developed world. Government debt almost doubled in a year. The level of debt among Irish households and companies was the highest in the European Union. The country's gross indebtedness was larger than Japan's, which has thirty times the population. The average Irish person owed €37,000.

Irish house prices had fallen more rapidly than any others in Europe. With a fifth of its office spaces empty, Dublin had the highest vacancy rate of any European capital and was rated as having the worst development and investment potential of twenty-seven European cities. The Irish stock exchange had fallen by 68 per cent in 2008 – a much more dramatic collapse than in other developed countries.

The average Irish family had lost almost half its financial assets, whose worth had fallen from €95,000 at the height of the boom in 2006 to €51,000 in mid-2009 – not counting the steep decline in the worth of its house. Unemployment rose faster than in any other Western European country, increasing by 85 per cent in a year. Ireland also ended up establishing a massive bad bank, the National Asset Management Agency (Nama), to take over €90 billion in loans to developers from banks that would otherwise be insolvent. This was another global number one for Ireland: Nama will hold more assets than any publicly quoted property company in the world, dwarfing giants such as GE Capital Real Estate and Morgan Stanley Real Estate, which own assets of €60 billion and €48 billion respectively.

In its rise and fall, Ireland made Icarus look boringly stable. The relationship of its recent past to its present was that of party to hangover – the headache was in direct proportion to the indulgence that preceded it. But the reversal of fortune in which the Celtic Tiger became a bedraggled alley cat was not simply an Irish concern. As Bertie Ahern's untimely posturing on the world stage demonstrated, the Irish economy was, for a full decade, the poster child of free-market globalisation. It was understood, not simply as the story of how one small and peripheral European country moved from relative poverty to prosperity, but as a moral tale with a happy ending for all those who learned its lessons. For most of the twentieth century, Ireland had struggled to be like other countries. But between the late 1990s and 2008, other countries were told they must struggle to be like Ireland.

This, ironically, was particularly true in the years when the Irish economy was most like Humpty Dumpty – bloated, fragile, sitting smugly at a great height and headed for a fall. In 2005, the official government publication *Lithuania in the World* announced that 'Lithuania is keen to repeat the economic growth story of Ireland, the Celtic Tiger'. In 2006, two centre-right Latvian parties, Latvia's Way and Latvia First, promised the electorate that they would follow the Irish path and raise living standards to Irish levels within a decade. In January 2007, the government of Trinidad hosted a seminar on 'The Irish Model of Economic Development – Lessons For Trinidad and Tobago'. The following August, the Americas Society and the US/Uruguay chamber of commerce heard a presentation on Ireland, concluding that the 'Irish model is a strategy that can work for other countries, irrespective of time and place'. Even as late as February 2008, the first minister of Scotland, Alex Salmond, was pledging that 'we will create a Celtic Lion economy to rival the Celtic Tiger across the Irish Sea'.

The crowning glory of the 'Irish model' arrived precisely at the moment when that model was tripping over its high heels and falling off the catwalk. For centuries, the Irish had dreamed of being like Americans – an ambition that millions of them fulfilled in the flesh. Then, in one of history's weirdest reversals, there was a moment when some Americans with a serious prospect of power began to dream of being more like Ireland. Not as in wearing Aran sweaters, drinking pints of Guinness and waxing lyrical in a charming brogue, but in real, serious economic terms.

In April 2008, Phil Gramm, the former Republican senator and economics adviser to presidential candidate John McCain, told *US News and World Report* that 'The only place socialism is seriously debated in the world is in Washington, DC . . . Ireland is a perfect example. Senator McCain's people immigrated from Ireland along with millions of others because they were hungry. Today, Ireland has among the lowest tax rates in the world, one of the best business climates in the world, and as a result they have overtaken Americans in per capita income.'

In September, McCain himself picked up the theme in one of his televised presidential campaign debates with Barack Obama: 'Right now, the United States of American business pays the second-highest business taxes in the world, 35 per cent. Ireland pays 11 per cent. Now, if you're a business person, and you can locate any place in the world, then, obviously, if you go to the country where it's 11 per cent tax versus 35 per cent, you're going to be able to create jobs, increase your business, make more investment, et cetera.'

McCain got the figures wrong (the corporation tax rate in Ireland is 12.5 per cent) and his timing was rotten: even as he spoke the Irish banking system was frantically trying to hide the scale of the bad loans to property developers that rendered it effectively insolvent. But in citing Ireland as the model that his presidency would follow, he was putting the final seal on the idea that this previously benighted island offered empirical proof that the way forward for everyone was extreme economic globalisation, low personal and corporate taxes, 'business-friendly' government and light regulation. The Irish formula was the new universal truth of economics, society and development. It transcended history and geography and, as the Uruguayans had been told, it worked 'irrespective of time and place'.

It had, indeed, defied geography by inserting the American way of doing business into Europe. Even sceptical Europeans began to believe this: in May 2008, an extensive article in *Le Monde* hailed Ireland as 'un "american dream" à l'européenne'.

The problem with this idea was not just that it was wrong or that it was believed by politicians and policy makers around the world. It was that the Irish themselves came to believe in it. They managed, collectively, to misunderstand why they became prosperous and in doing so to waste and eventually to destroy that prosperity. The rise and fall of the Celtic Tiger was indeed a kind of moral tale, but the lesson was not that free-market globalisation is a panacea for the world's ills. It is, on the contrary, that politics, society, morality and collective institutions matter.

There is no doubt that Ireland's economic performance in the late 1990s was genuinely remarkable. The rate of unemployment in the fifteen European Union countries as a whole remained more or less static throughout the 1990s. In Ireland, it was cut in half, from a desperately high 15.6 per cent to 7.4 per cent (and shortly afterwards to less than 5 per cent). The level of consistent poverty fell from 15 per cent of the population to 5 per cent. In 1986, Irish GDP per head of population was a miserable two-thirds of the EU average, and even in 1991 it was just over three-quarters. In 1999, it was 111 per cent of the average, and significantly higher than that of the UK.

The Irish share of foreign investment by US-based corporations rose from 2 per cent to 7 per cent. By 2000, Ireland had $38,000 of foreign investment for every man, woman and child – more than six times the EU average. World-leading corporations like Pfizer (which makes all of its Viagra in County Cork) or Intel (whose European base is in County Kildare) created good, well-paid and increasingly highly skilled jobs.

This was a new way for a country to get rich: Ireland became far more dependent on foreign investment for its manufacturing base than almost any other society. By 1999, half the manufacturing jobs were in foreign-based companies compared to 20 per cent for the EU as a whole. But it seemed to work. At the end of the 1990s, Ireland had become the largest exporter of computer software in the world. The overall value of exports more than doubled between 1995 and 2000. In the ten years to 2004, the growth of Irish national income averaged over 7 per cent, more than double that of the USA and almost triple the average growth rate in the eurozone.

Mass emigration, with all of its debilitating economic, social and psychological effects, ended and was gradually replaced by large-scale immigration – a phenomenon that had been utterly unimaginable to generations of Irish people. Coming to Ireland to look for work would have been, at the start of the 1990s, like going to the Sahara for the skiing. By the time of the 2006 census, a tenth of those living in Ireland were born elsewhere.

Partly as a result of these two factors, the population rose at a phenomenal rate. While the rest of the EU added one person to every 1,000 between 1998 and 2008, Ireland added ten. For a country in which depopulation had been the ultimate mark of despair, the simple fact that there were a lot more people around was a historical achievement.

All of this was great, and it was also a lot of fun. Coinciding with the gradual establishment of peace in Northern Ireland after the Good Friday agreements of 1998, it made Irish people feel a lot better about themselves. Ireland shook off much of its authoritarian religiosity and became a more open and tolerant society. The pall of failure that had hung over the Irish state for most of its independent existence seemed to have been blown away for ever. Ireland was young, buoyant and energetic, and to those who complained that older spiritual values were being lost, the ready answer was that having a job and a house and a choice about staying in your own country can be pretty spiritually uplifting too. Even the undertone of hysteria in the increasingly frantic consumer spending could be forgiven – Irish people had been relatively deprived for a long time and were now working at least as hard as they played.

Yet the very speed of the transformation contained its own problems. There was little time to absorb what had happened, to weigh it and understand it. How much of it was about Ireland and how much a mere side-effect of a global boom? How much was due to good policy decisions and how much was sheer dumb luck? It was easier to adopt a simple explanation that had the virtue of chiming with what the rest of the world (and especially those parts of it most committed to the dominant free-market ideology) wanted Ireland to prove.

A narrative emerged. Fianna Fáil and the Progressive Democrats came to power in 1997, with the PDs (supported by the Fianna Fáil Minister for Finance, Charlie McCreevy) pulling the centre of gravity of Irish governance sharply to the right. Income taxes were cut, foreign companies were courted with massive tax breaks and the promise of light regulation. Enterprise was encouraged and rewarded (or, in plainer words, the rich were idolised and allowed to avoid petty restrictions like paying tax). The power of free-market globalisation was unleashed and Ireland became a large-scale version of a TV makeover show, with the 'before' pictures showing a slovenly, depressed wretch and the 'after' images a smiling, bling-bedecked beauty, who went on to start her own self-improvement course for similarly abject little countries.

It was a good story, and like most good stories, it was mostly untrue. The reality is that far from being a model that could be applied 'irrespective of time and place', the Celtic Tiger was the product of a very specific place at a very particular time. A lot of things came together in Ireland in the mid-1990s, and not many of them had much to do with the application of free-market orthodoxy.

For a start, one of the reasons the Irish economy grew so fast after 1995 is that it had grown so slowly before that. The performance of the Irish economy since independence in 1922, and especially during the post-war boom that transformed the rest of Western Europe in the 1950s, was utterly miserable. Cormac O Grada and Kevin O'Rourke noted of Irish economic performance from the end of the Second World War until 1988 that the country was a 'dramatic underperformer during this period', a 'spectacular outlier' and 'the sick man of Europe'. As the historian Joe Lee noted in 1989, 'No other European country, east or west, north or south, for which remotely reliable evidence exists, had recorded so slow a rate of growth of national income in the twentieth century.' Much of what happened in the 1990s was simply that Ireland caught up with the living standards of the region it belongs to – Western Europe – and got to where it should have been all along. The energy unleashed by the process of catching up, combined with the advantages of not having an old heavy industrial base, allowed Ireland (temporarily) to outperform those European neighbours. In a longer perspective, all that was happening was a regional levelling-out.

A second factor was the long global boom of the 1990s. The growth in world economic output between 1995 and 1998 exceeded that during the entire 10,000-year period from the dawn of agriculture to the start of the twentieth century. The growth of the world economy in 1997 alone far exceeded what was achieved during the entire seventeeth century. As part of this trade-fuelled boom, American companies invested more money abroad in the 1990s than in the entire previous four decades. Half of their investment of $750 billion went to Europe. It is not a wonder that a small but significant slice was invested in Ireland, a stable, Anglophone country with EU membership, relatively low wages and a well-educated workforce. It would, in fact, have been truly amazing if this had not happened. To put it another way, if Ireland hadn't experienced rapid economic growth during the extraordinary global investment boom of the 1990s, the case for letting it sink beneath the Atlantic waves would have been unanswerable.

There were other key factors that are not dreamt of in free-market philosophy. Some of them were rooted specifically in progressive politics. Feminism, for example – the Irish women's liberation movement began in the early 1970s and involved a long struggle against the control of female sexuality and reproduction by the Catholic Church and Fianna Fáil. (The sale of contraceptives, for example, was not fully legalised until 1992.) Paradoxically, the Ireland of the 1990s reaped enormous economic benefits both from the repression of women before the 1970s and from their subsequent relative liberation. The old culture produced a demographic boom – Irish fertility had been startlingly high well into the 1980s, with the result that there were a lot of youngsters around in the 1990s. At the same time, however, those fertility rates dropped dramatically as women gained more freedom, allowing ever larger numbers of mothers to join or stay in the paid workforce.

Together, these factors had a lot to do with the creation of the boom. There were simply a lot more people in a position to earn money. In 1986, every ten workers in Ireland supported 22 people who were too young or too old to work, who were women working in the home, or who were unemployed. By 1999, those ten workers were supporting just fourteen dependants, and by 2005, just five. With a grim irony, Ireland was also reaping the economic benefits of mass emigration in the 1950s, which meant that many of the elderly people who should have been in Ireland were actually in the UK and elsewhere and being cared for by other societies.

As well as feminism, the Irish boom was fuelled in part by another progressive force of which free-market conservatives tend not to be overly fond: social democracy. Ireland was blessed that the kind of right-wing populist politics it practised at home was not in vogue in Europe for much of the 1990s. A good, old-fashioned French socialist, Jacques Delors, was president of the European Commission. Citing quaint notions like solidarity and equality, he oversaw a doubling of the EU's regional, social and structural funds, of which Ireland was the most obvious beneficiary. The whole of Ireland was declared a disadvantaged area and the EU poured in IR£8.6 billion in aid between 1987 and 1998.

These structural funds alone accounted for 2.6 per cent of Ireland's Gross National Product during the 1990s, giving a crucial lift to growth and in particular funding the infrastructural developments without which that growth would have quickly stalled. Perhaps more importantly, by underwriting Irish agriculture through the Common Agricultural Policy, the EU allowed rural Ireland to accept a sugar-coated version of modernity, ensuring that Ireland could transform itself socially without significant instability. All of this was classic Big government interventionism – the precise opposite of what free-market ideologists like Phil Gramm and his local imitators would have decreed.

Lastly, Irish governments themselves did two things to make the boom possible, and the very mention of either of them would have caused the average Republican senator in the US to call for an exorcism. One was to invest heavily in the expansion of state-funded third-level education. A rare reason to be cheerful after the bursting of the Irish bubble was that 42.3 per cent of the population aged 25–34 had completed third-level education, the second highest rate in the EU. The other intervention was the construction of a highly sophisticated system of social partnership in which the state, employers, trade unions and other social actors agreed frameworks, not just for wages, but for national policy on a range of issues. This process had its weaknesses and limitations but it did ensure a remarkable level of industrial peace and helped to create a consensus around basic social and economic goals.

With the exception of social partnership, which he managed with consummate skill, none of this had much to do with Bertie Ahern or the government he led to power in 1997. Ahern in fact inherited the boom from the previous Fine Gael/Labour administration: exports had started to rise rapidly in 1993, and by the time Ahern took office had already doubled in five years. In 1997, Ireland had already reached the average EU level of GDP per head of population. Short of some global disaster, the overwhelming likelihood was that Irish economic growth would continue under its own steam.

The questions that the ruling trio of Ahern, McCreevy and the PD leader Mary Harney really faced were about how the money that was now flowing into the state coffers should be used and how the economy could become successful in the long term, beyond the inevitable succession of bust to boom. They had an opportunity that was unique in Irish history. They had the resources to invest in the creation of a decent society, one that would be economically, socially and environmentally sustainable. They had a population that was optimistic, self-confident and ready for a challenge. They had incredibly favourable global conditions.

And they blew it. They allowed an unreconstructed culture of cronyism, self-indulgence and, at its extremes, of outright corruption, to remain in place, with fatal long-term consequences. They fostered, alongside the real economy in which people created goods and sold them, a false economy of facades and fictions. They practised the economics of utter idiocy, watching a controlled explosion of growth turn into a mad conflagration and aiming petrol-filled pressure-hoses at the raging flames. They amused themselves with fantasy lifestyles and pet projects while the opportunity to break cycles of deprivation and end child poverty was frittered away. They turned self-confidence into arrogance, optimism into swagger, aspiration into self-delusion.

And they did this because they bought in to the fallacy that the Irish had somehow discovered a 'model of development' that would work anytime, anywhere. Instead of the complex social, historical and political processes – and the sheer good fortune – that had created the Celtic Tiger, they had captured a genie whose golden lamp need only be stroked to ensure success. The formula was ultimately simple – be nice to the rich. Give capital its head, don't stand in its way and it will work its magic. Let the wealthy become ever more wealthy and everyone will benefit. The tragedy was not that Ireland's rulers and their cheerleaders chanted this mantra. It was that they actually believed in it.

This self-delusion became stronger as the Celtic Tiger boom was actually petering out. In essence, the real boom lasted from 1995 until 2001. What made it real were two forces that were not at all magical and could be precisely measured: sharp rises in output per worker (productivity) and in manufacturing exports. Both of these forces began to wind down in the new millennium. Productivity growth between 2000 and 2006 slowed to its lowest level since 1980. It was half what it had been in the classic boom years and actually slipped below the average for the developed (OECD) economies. By 2008, Irish productivity levels were below the OECD average.

So was the level of growth in Irish exports. Ireland's total share of the world's trade in goods, which had risen steadily from the mid-1990s, peaked in 2002 and then started to decline every year. While there was a steady rise in the export of services (especially of financial services), it was more than offset by the fall in the share of trade in tangible merchandise. Between 2000 and 2006, the number of manufacturing jobs in Ireland actually declined by about 20,000 – a fall masked by large rises in the numbers at work in construction and the public services.

Up to the turn of the century, Ireland's overall balance of payments (national income minus national expenditure) was just marginally in the red, and in 2003 the country pretty much broke even. Thereafter, though, the downhill slope was like something from the Winter Olympics and by 2007, the country was €10 billion in the red. This huge gap was being filled by equally enormous levels of borrowing.

None of this was disastrous in itself. The boom had given Ireland a historic opportunity. There was money in the government coffers. There were more and more people at work. The demographics were uniquely favourable. The air of depression and inferiority had been banished. What was needed was a vision of how a boom could be shaped into a steady and socially just kind of prosperity.

At this point, the creation of decent public services and of an equal and inclusive society should not have been mere afterthoughts to the creation of wealth. On the contrary, the sustainable generation of wealth itself demanded investment in innovation, creativity and cohesion. That, in turn meant investment in people – health, education, childcare, affordable housing.

What made the real end of the Celtic Tiger after 2001 disastrous, however, was the decision of the Fianna Fáil-led government to replace one kind of growth with another. Ireland had become prosperous because its workers were unusually productive and because its economy was exporting goods that people wanted to buy. The government decided that it would stay prosperous by going for what the National Competitiveness Council would later call 'growth derived from asset price inflation, fuelled by a combination of low interest rates, reckless lending and speculation'. Being prosperous would be replaced by feeling rich. Consumption would replace production. Building would replace manufacturing as the engine of growth. The nation was to think of itself as a lottery winner, the blessed recipient of a staggering windfall. It was to spend, spend, spend. And understanding what had happened and how it could be sustained was much less important than the manic need to keep growing, and spending, at all costs.

Stupidity and corruption shaped this process.

The role of sheer idiocy should not be understated. As finance minister, Charlie McCreevy's credo was a textbook statement of macroeconomic illiteracy: 'When I have the money, I spend it, when I don't have it, I don't spend it.' This childish mantra, obliterating at a stroke everything that governments worldwide had learned about the need to restrain a runaway economy by spending less and boost a flagging one by spending more, was the economic equivalent of bulimia: binge and purge, binge and purge. Much of the binging was breathtakingly brainless, with money thrown at pet projects or vote-catching exercises without any attempt to analyse the costs and benefits. It was McCreevy who announced medical cards for all those over seventy, giving free GP services and prescriptions, on the basis of a back-of-the-envelope calculation that it would cover 39,000 people at a cost of €19 million. In fact, in the first year, it covered 63,000 at a cost of €126 million. It was he who announced, with no costing and no detail, the folly of the so-called 'decentralisation' of government departments and agencies to provincial towns which meant, for example, buying five large sites at the height of the property boom for €16 million and allowing them to lie idle indefinitely, and a running total of €230 million spent on the schemes by 2008. Both of these policies were straightforward pre-election gimmicks.

And all of this was done in a way that was deliberately socially regressive. McCreevy made sure that the boom would preserve the deep inequalities in Irish society by using his budgets to redistribute income upwards. His budget for the year 2000, for example, made the incomes of the poorest 20 per cent of the population rise by less than 1 per cent, those of the middle-income groups rise by 2–3 per cent, and those in the top 30 per cent by about 4 per cent.

McCreevy gave priority to tax cuts over everything else. The cumulative effect was to create a fantasy land in which taxes could be cut while public spending was rising. People were encouraged to think that they didn't have to make choices – lavishly wasteful public expenditure didn't matter because no one had to pay for it. And the long-term effect of pumping all of this money into the economy through tax cuts and an artificial property boom was a massive rise in inflation which seriously damaged economic competitiveness. Inflation under McCreevy rose at twice the rate of Ireland's EU partners. Prices in Ireland in 2004 were 28 per cent above what they were when McCreevy took office in 1997; the corresponding figure for the EU was 14 per cent.

This stupidity was not about a lack of intelligence: McCreevy, Harney and Ahern were all very bright people. It was induced by a lethal cocktail of global ideology and Irish habits. On the one side, so-called free market ideology held government in contempt. When McCreevy boasted of spending money when he had it and not spending it when he didn't, he was expressing a deeply held belief that it was not the business of governments to interfere, for good or ill, in the workings of the economy. More broadly, if you believe, in accordance with the doctrines that dominated official thinking, that government itself is essentially evil, the very idea of using political power to effect the long-term transformation of a society is anathema.

On the other side, there was the ingrained Irish political habit of thinking only in the short term. Fianna Fáil in particular existed as a machine for the gaining and holding of power. It was in general inimical to political ideas that could be spelled out in detail or tested against reality. If ideas had to be worn at all, they could also be easily discarded. Bertie Ahern brought the party's contempt for coherent political values to new heights. This was a man who declared himself a socialist in 2004, having told his biographers six years earlier that 'I don't believe in all that socialist stuff. I've never met a socialist in my life'. This free and easy way with ideas meant that there could not be, from the top, any kind of vision for how Irish society should develop. When Ahern remarked, of his dream for a €1 billion white elephant sports stadium on the far outskirts of Dublin (quickly dubbed 'the Bertie Bowl'), that it would be the legacy of the Celtic Tiger, he betrayed the staggering poverty of social ambition that underlay the second phase of the Irish boom.

McCreevy and Harney were not personally corrupt, but Ahern saw nothing wrong with accepting large sums of cash from businessmen. In general, the government did not just

tolerate low standards in public life and business by doing little to challenge them. It preserved the attitudes that kept
them in place. In doing so, it failed to alter the well-estab-
lished climate of financial adventurism, in which recklessness
was encouraged by impunity. An atmosphere of insider intimacy in which cronyism thrived continued to hang over
boomtime Ireland. On their own, either political stupidity or
a tolerance for sleaze would have threatened the sustainability of the Irish economic miracle. Together, they ensured its
demise.

Jonathan Swift, in leaving money in his will for the found-
ing of a mental hospital in Dublin, noted that 'no nation
needed it so much'. The government adapted Swift's satire to
its own exercise in insanity:

> We used up all the wealth we had
> To build a ship for fools and mad
> And, knowing it proof against all shocks,
> Steered it blithely towards the rocks.

A Patriot for Me

'Thanks very much and I'll sort you out'
– Bertie Ahern to donor Barry English

For once in his political life, Bertie Ahern was entirely unequivocal. His mastery of the arts of evasion and ambiguity had once caused a frustrated opponent, Joe Higgins, to compare the task of getting a straight answer from him to 'playing handball against a haystack'. This time there was no masking of his true feelings, none of the babble of barely connected words that often left his listeners unsure about almost everything, not least whether the man was an idiot or a genius. This time, he was direct, eloquent and so sincere that not even the greatest sceptic could doubt that the tears in his eyes and the catch in his throat were involuntary symptoms of powerful emotion.

And so, in June 2006, Bertie Ahern stood at the graveside of his master, Charles Haughey, in Saint Fintan's Cemetery in Sutton and called him 'a patriot to his fingertips': 'The definition of a patriot is someone who devotes all their energy to the betterment of their countrymen. Charles Haughey was a patriot to his fingertips.' The catch in his voice came in his peroration when he referred to Haughey as 'Charlie, Boss', pausing for effect between the two terms, so that the second gathered its full resonance as a tribal act of homage to the lost leader.

But before then he had managed to articulate with some

precision the message that was to go forth from the grave-side: 'When the shadows have faded the light of his achievements will remain.' Those shadows were cast, of course, by the towering skyscrapers of money that the Boss had accumulated while holding high political office: the equivalent in 2006 of about €45 million, or 171 times his total salary payments as a full-time politician. Corruption, Ahern was saying, even on such a heroic scale, was of little long-term consequence. This was a serving Taoiseach, speaking at a formal state funeral (which cost the taxpayer at least €500,000, including €35,000 for food and drink for the invited guests). He was affirming as official policy the idea that theft, deception and fraud on a grand scale were relatively minor matters in Ireland.

For most of the previous decade, since his grandiose crookery was first confirmed by the report of the McCracken tribunal of inquiry in 1997, Haughey had been treated as Fianna Fáil's reprobate uncle, a family embarrassment whose scandalous behaviour should not, however, be held against the present generation. The state funeral was, however, a calculated act of contrition for these attempts to distance the party from the Boss. This act of collective homage was solemnised by the party's young princeling, the future Minister for Finance, Brian Lenihan – son, namesake and political heir of one of Haughey's closest allies. Haughey had stolen €250,000 from a fund set up to pay for a liver transplant for Lenihan's father, whom Haughey described as 'one of my closest personal friends and certainly my closest political friend'. In a sign that even this was to be forgiven and forgotten, Lenihan did the first reading at Haughey's funeral Mass. It was a potent statement of the official ethic – you could steal from your friend's life-saving medical fund and still be a patriot right down to the tips of the fingers that were elegantly snaffling the banknotes.

This was an important moral statement – for Bertie Ahern himself, who clearly liked to imagine that his own venality in public office would be forgotten in time, and for some of the other mourners. Among them, for example, was the builder and developer Mick Bailey who, with his brother Tom, owned Bovale Developments, one of the largest private landowners in Ireland. On the day of Haughey's funeral, and conscious perhaps that much of the nation's attention would be focused on that event, the Bailey brothers quietly acknowledged that they had made probably the largest single tax settlement in the history of the state – €22 million to cover systematic tax evasion since 1983.

The Bailey brothers, in fact, embodied the culture of impunity that is the most distinctive aspect of Irish corruption. Political sleaze in various forms is endemic in many democratic societies. Where Ireland differs from almost all other developed societies, however, Italy being the obvious exception, is that no price need be paid for getting caught. Haughey was never prosecuted either for stealing money from the public purse (and from Fianna Fáil itself) or for lying about it to a tribunal of inquiry. Nor was he, in Fianna Fáil's worldview, ultimately dishonoured by the revelation of his criminality. And when this is so for those at the very top, the infection cannot be quarantined.

Mick and Tom Bailey were key figures in the Irish property and construction business, whose land-bank alone was worth €51 million in 2002 and had probably doubled in value by 2006. They were also key figures in the corrupt relationship between that business and politics. In 1989, Mick wrote to James Gogarty of the structural engineering company JMSE telling him that he could 'procure' a majority of the members of Dublin County Council to vote for the re-zoning of over 700 acres of agricultural land in North Dublin that JMSE owned so that it could be developed for housing. The ultimate publication of that letter led to the establishment of a tribunal of inquiry chaired by Mr Justice Flood.

That inquiry found Mick Bailey to be directly involved in bribery. In June 1989, he handed over either IR£30,000 or IR£40,000 to the Fianna Fáil minister Ray Burke as part of a bribe of either IR£60,000 or IR£80,000 to help get the lands re-zoned for development. He also made three payments totalling between IR£16,000 and IR£20,000 to a senior planning official, the assistant Dublin city and county manager George Redmond.

Both Mick and Tom Bailey also lied under oath at the Flood tribunal. In its report, the inquiry found that Mick Bailey had given 'false evidence' about a meeting with Ray Burke. He lied about money he had allegedly given to James Gogarty. He leaked information to the *Sunday Independent* newspaper and then claimed that he couldn't co-operate with the tribunal because of his fear of leaks. He was also found to have given false evidence under oath in relation to meetings and dealings with George Redmond, including the payment of bribes.

Tom Bailey made a false allegation under oath about money he had given to James Gogarty. He also failed to provide the tribunal with financial records even when it obtained an order of discovery against him. Not only did Mick and Tom Bailey each give false evidence under oath, but the tribunal found that they had colluded together to tell the same lies. As the taxing master of the High Court put it in refusing to pay their legal costs, the Baileys engaged in 'a deliberate attempt to ensure that the tribunal would never find the truth'. There are laws against this kind of thing, even in Ireland.

In almost any other democracy, it would be extraordinary for those who engaged in long-term tax evasion, bribery of public officials, giving false evidence under oath and obstructing a public inquiry not to be prosecuted for all of these offences. It would be utterly unthinkable for them not to be prosecuted for any of them. Yet the Baileys were never charged with any offence, suffered no civil sanctions (such as being declared unfit to continue as company directors) and continued to be lent large sums of money by Irish banks.

Not only, however, were the Bailey brothers not prosecuted, but they were still able to mingle cheerily and intimately with Bertie Ahern and members of his cabinet. Less than two months after Haughey's funeral and the revelation of the Baileys' vast evasion of taxes, Tom Bailey was one of the guests paying €400 a head for the chance to mingle with the Taoiseach and government ministers in the Fianna Fáil tent at the Galway races.

At worst, the Bailey brothers' walks on the wild side were the subject of political in-jokes. His most famous saying was his reply to a question posed by James Gogarty as they were on their way to hand the bribes to Ray Burke: 'Will we get a receipt?' 'Will we fuck!' In 2009, the former Minister of State at the Department of Finance Tom Parlon was overheard regaling his friends at the Galway rces with a hilarious anecdote: 'Tom Bailey has a horse running and I asked him "Will he win?" and he said "Will he fuck!".'

Parlon could hardly be accused of bad taste because he was telling a kind of truth: public ethics in Ireland were a joke. The paradox of Irish political culture in the Celtic Tiger years was that revelations of corruption didn't make things better, they made them worse. In the 1980s and early 1990s, when anyone with a sense of smell could get a ripe hum of rottenness off figures like Haughey and Burke, glimpses of whose dubious financial dealings occasionally emerged through the fog of Ireland's heavily restrictive libel laws, it was possible to believe that if ever there were incontrovertible proof of their venality, the system would be shaken to its core. The assumption was that some kind of rough morality actually operated, and that wrongdoing, once revealed, would be punished. The old culture would not survive, and if Fianna Fáil itself were to do so, it would have to be thoroughly reformed.

What actually happened, however, was something much stranger and ultimately much more damaging. From the mid-1990s onwards, it became ever more undeniable that corruption was deeply embedded, both at the top and the bottom of Irish public life. A deep but vague unease was gradually replaced with facts and figures, offshore accounts and lodgements, givers and takers. Three major figures – Haughey and Burke from Fianna Fáil and Michael Lowry, a minister for the major Opposition party Fine Gael – were caught bang to rights. A largely successful conspiracy to control the development of the capital city by systematically bribing large numbers of Fianna Fáil and Fine Gael councillors was uncovered. It became completely clear that the public interest was being literally sold out to an inner circle of businessmen.

Sleazy as these crimes were, they were not unique to Irish politics. What was peculiar to Ireland, however, was what happened next – virtually nothing. Burke was briefly jailed for Revenue offences. Liam Lawlor, the Fianna Fáil fixer who had a way of turning up whenever there was blurry work at the crossroads of money and politics, went to prison for refusing to co-operate with a tribunal of inquiry. Frank Dunlop, the former Fianna Fáil government press secretary turned local government 'lobbyist' and bagman, eventually got an 18-month sentence for bribing councillors to re-zone land and make developers rich. George Redmond, the planning official found by the tribunal to have been bribed by Mick Bailey and others, was arrested with £300,000 in cash and stockbroker cheques as he was stepping off a flight from the Isle of Man, and served almost a year in jail. But that conviction was quashed and charges against Redmond were subsequently dropped.

There was, however, no real change in the political culture. No one was actually prosecuted for paying bribes – rich people like the Baileys who benefited from corruption were entirely untouched. Perhaps more importantly, the Irish electorate showed an extraordinary degree of tolerance towards politicians who were known to have engaged in dodgy dealings. One of the key assumptions behind the idea that revelations would change the system was that voters would not want to elect such people. It was sadly naive.

What happened was not that the majority of people disbelieved the evidence of corruption and went on innocently trusting their politicians. On the contrary, public trust in politicians almost evaporated. An *Irish Times* poll of women in 2007 found that just 2 per cent said they 'completely' trusted politicians in the Dáil, with a further 19 per cent trusting them 'somewhat'. The Diageo Quality of Life surveys found that 9 per cent trusted the government a great deal to be honest and fair in 2001, and the figure fell to 3 per cent in 2004. With belief in the honesty and fairness of government becoming a crank theory, like believing that aliens are controlling our thoughts or that Freemasons are running the world, it might seem incredible that voters continued to elect the same politicians. Yet the truth was that many voters didn't greatly care.

Civic morality is not absent in Ireland, but it is marginal and fragile. The political system is tribal, local and clientelist – there is a strong impulse to vote, not for a decent person or a national leader, but for someone who will successfully manipulate the system on behalf of both constituents individually and the constituency as a whole. If morality comes into the equation it is often through the vague but powerful feeling that a lack of it might make for a more effective local champion. Thus, Ray Burke got his highest ever vote in North Dublin in 1977 – after the *Sunday Independent* and *Hibernia* magazine had shown that he had received a bribe of £15,000 from the builders Brennan and McGowan. (There was a Garda investigation but it went nowhere.)

The most spectacular example of this phenomenon in the Celtic Tiger years was the electoral career of Michael Lowry. Lowry had to resign as Minister for Transport, Energy and Communications in 1996 when it emerged that a client of his refrigeration business, Dunnes Stores, had paid for a huge extension to his house – an obvious tax evasion scam. At the 1997 general election, he got an extra 4,000 votes in North Tipperary.

It then became completely clear that Lowry was a cheat and a liar. The McCracken tribunal revealed his evasion of taxes to be complex, organised and large-scale. His company Garuda under-declared both VAT and PAYE, and eventually had to cough up €1.2 million after a Revenue audit. He also diddled his personal taxes, and settled for almost €200,000.

A key part of his business arrangement with Dunnes Stores was described in the McCracken report as 'a sham' put in place to avoid taxes.

Lowry's lies were legion. He lied to the Revenue when he availed of a tax amnesty in 1993 without declaring all his hidden income – an absolute condition for getting the benefit of the amnesty. (It says much for the standards in Irish public life that Lowry actually told his party leader John Bruton, whose personal integrity is not in doubt, that he had availed of the amnesty – and thus that he had been cheating on his taxes – but was appointed to the cabinet anyway.)

He misled the Dáil in December 1996 by failing to mention a series of large payments from Dunnes. He told the Dáil that if he had been trying to hide money he would have 'put it in an offshore account', creating the impression that he had no such account. In fact, he had at least four: one in the Bank of Ireland in the Isle of Man; one in an Allied Irish Bank subsidiary in Jersey; another Isle of Man account held through a company called Badgeworth; and an Irish Nationwide Isle of Man account. Only the first two of these accounts were disclosed to the McCracken tribunal – the existence of the other two emerged at the later Moriarty tribunal.

He indignantly denied in the Dáil that 'my house in Carysfort, Blackrock, was somehow financed in an irregular way'. In fact the house was bought in trust for Lowry by a developer and the money for its extensive refurbishment was routed through the Isle of Man Nationwide account and came from a loan to him from an executive of the giant Smurfit packaging corporation.

Lowry, moreover, has shown no real remorse. He has never apologised. He regards himself, as he told the *Sunday*

Independent in 2009, as 'a victim of my own success', whose only fault was to 'stick my head too high above the parapet'. He sees himself as a target of 'state oppression' who was 'only judged by the hobnobs'. (Whether the hobnobs in question were of the plain or chocolate-coated variety remains, at the time of writing, unclear.)

And why not? Mr Justice McCracken pointed to the damage done by 'the public perception that a person in the position of a government minister and member of cabinet was able to ignore, and indeed cynically evade, both the taxation and exchange control laws of the state with impunity'. But that impunity remained in place – Lowry has never been prosecuted for his breaches of those laws.

What happened after the McCracken report? Lowry stood for election again. His effrontery was entirely vindicated: he topped the poll and was elected on the first count. In the 2007 general election, after the Moriarty tribunal had spent many of the intervening years investigating allegations that Lowry, as minister, had fixed the competition for a mobile phone licence, his vote went up again: to a poll-topping 13,000.

Even when politicians were actually prosecuted and convicted of fraud (an event that makes the lunar azure glow seem commonplace), there was no evidence that it did their electoral prospects any harm. In the 2009 local elections, when the disastrous consequences of the refusal to take public ethics seriously ought to have been obvious, two convicted fraudsters were elected.

In 2002, a former Fianna Fáil candidate in Sligo, Michael Clarke, was convicted of handling stolen cheques and conspiring to steal a cheque. Clarke had conspired with an official from the Department of Agriculture to cash cheques from the department made out to fictitious individuals supposedly involved in a dairy hygiene scheme. After serving his two-year prison sentence, Clarke ran in the 2009 local elections and topped the poll. He explained his success as a matter of trust: 'People were very kind to me on the doors. They know they can trust me and everything they say to me will remain confidential.'

In the same election, this time in Galway, Michael 'Stroke' Fahy also topped the poll. Just six months earlier he, too, had been convicted of stealing public money – from the very county council on which he served – by using public workers and funds to erect fencing around his home. The judge in his case called on Fahy 'to act with honour and resign his seat'. The concept was clearly not one he found easy to fathom. As with Clarke, a criminal conviction actually seemed to increase his appeal. Clarke had failed to win a seat before he went to jail; Fahy significantly increased his vote after being found guilty. When a puzzled local asked on a local internet discussion forum why his neighbours had voted for Fahy ('I simply find it incomprehensible that corrupt politicians can be elected and re-elected') the reply was that 'people feel he was wrongly sent to jail, a middle-aged man caring for his mother sent to Castlerea prison for a bit of fencing around the house – a joke'. The real wonder was not that fraudsters got elected but that more politicians did not claim to be crooks in order to get elected. There had been a time in Ireland when it was a political asset to have served time behind bars for Sinn Féin. In the Celtic Tiger era, it was an asset to have been behind bars for Mé Féin.

In most countries, breaking the laws you helped to pass or defrauding the public body on which you served would be seen as exacerbating factors in a crime. In Ireland, bizarrely, they seem to be accepted as mitigating factors. People who were generally in favour of letting all kinds of criminals rot in hell somehow became bleeding-heart liberals when the criminals were politicians. Instead of locking them up and throwing away the key, they were all in favour of care in the community, preferably in the safe and supportive environment of a parliament or county council.

Why did this attitude prevail? The localism and clientelism of Irish politics was a large factor. Politicians were elected, not necessarily to implement impersonal policies or standards, but to provide a service both to individual constituents and to the constituency as a whole. Helping a voter to get a local authority house or the area as a whole to get a new road or school covered a multitude of sins. Oddly enough, the extreme experience of globalisation in Ireland may have enhanced these factors. As a reaction to the idea of faceless, fluid forces shaping one's destiny, an extreme of local loyalty and of personal intimacy ('a middle-aged man caring for his mother') is an act of defiance against Them – whoever they are. Doing the last thing you're supposed to do may be the final assertion of power against a feeling of powerlessness.

There was, however, another reason for this reaction – bizarrely, the revelations and inquiries themselves. Because knowledge did not lead to action and the same system remained in place, the ultimate impact of the certainty that there was deep corruption in Irish politics was cynicism about politics itself. Voters got to watch their leaders developing unfortunate memory loss in sworn inquiries. They saw the operation of *omertà*, as big political players were protected and defended by their colleagues while the small fry were abandoned to their fate. They witnessed the ruthlessness with which loyalties were abandoned or restored, as a figure like Haughey went from paragon to pariah to patriot, as the Party's needs dictated. Instead of raising standards, the revelations inadvertently lowered them. The broad public response to the stripping away of the illusions of patriotism and public service was the belief that all politics are corrupt. Politicians, in the favoured cliché, were 'in it for themselves'.

This was patently untrue, but it was not an irrational response to a situation in which outright racketeering is revealed at the highest levels of state and nothing really happens. And what flowed logically from it was the bizarre notion that, since they were all corrupt, anyone who was actually caught was simply being singled out by those evil biscuits, Michael Lowry's 'hobnobs'. Why were they going after a good Tipperary man when there were so many rogues in Dublin? Why were they blaming poor Stroke Fahy, who was good to his ancient mother, for stealing a bit of fencing off the council when Charlie Haughey was 'a patriot to his fingergtips'?

What happened was a perverse application of the conclusion that Mr Justice McCracken had reached in his report in 1997. McCracken wrote of Lowry that 'If such a person can behave in this way without serious sanctions being imposed, it becomes very difficult to condemn others who similarly flout the law'. The good judge's assumption was presumably that Lowry and others like him would be punished and that basic standards of morality and legality would be laid down once and for all. With impunity for Lowry, Haughey and vastly wealthy businessmen like the Bailey brothers, that assumption was turned on its head. How, indeed, could anyone be condemned for flouting the law (unless of course they were drawn from the usual reservoir of poverty and chaos that was regularly drained into the prisons) when some of the most egregious political criminals got away with it?

It took a little while for those in power (in effect, Fianna Fáil) to understand what was going on. In the early years of the corruption revelations, Fianna Fáil felt the need to be seen to be taking a tough line, not just on those who accepted bribes, but on those who gave them and enriched themselves as a result. In the party manifesto for the 2002 election, and subsequently in the Programme for Government, Fianna Fáil promised that it would introduce 'a Proceeds of Corruption Act modelled on the proceeds of crime legislation, to further target white-collar crime and corruption in both public and private sectors'. After the Flood tribunal report, Bertie Ahern put flesh on these bones: the Corruption Assets Bureau would 'recover assets corruptly obtained and . . . recover any increase in the value of an asset that has been obtained through corruption . . . Those who benefit from corrupting public officials and those holding elective office must, in addition to criminal sanctions, be held financially accountable. Such persons must be hit where it hurts most – in their pockets.'

Did the Corruption Assets Bureau get established? For an answer the reader is referred to Mick Bailey's famous response to James Gogarty(?). Gradually, encouraged by the evidence of public support for fraudsters and tax dodgers, Fianna Fáil began to realise that it did not in fact have to do anything that might upset its own wealthy supporters. It really was possible to get away with it.

The starkest consequence of this attitude was that it continued to be acceptable, within Fianna Fáil at least, for senior politicians to accept money from wealthy private individuals. This became clear in the party's reaction to the gradual revelation of the strange state of Bertie Ahern's own finances. The Mahon tribunal, successor to the Flood inquiry, looking into an allegation that Ahern had accepted money from the Cork-based property developer Owen O'Callaghan (a claim both men vigorously denied), found itself examining bank lodgements and other transactions totalling IR£452,800 – the equivalent in 2008 of €886,830. These lodgements – some of them in sterling and therefore almost certainly not from his salary – were made to Ahern's accounts in the period between 1988 and 1997. In that respect Fianna Fáil could claim that they represented an old pre-Celtic Tiger political culture. The problem was that, as they began to be revealed from 2006 onwards, not one senior figure in Fianna Fáil, least of all Ahern himself, managed to state that the acceptance by a senior minister (Ahern was Minister for Finance for much of the period in question) of private donations was unequivocally wrong.

The best that Ahern could manage in relation to his acceptance of two supposed 'dig-outs' from businessmen was that they represented 'an error of judgment' because they were 'capable of misinterpretation'. (The real problem therefore being, of course, the bad-mindedness of the misinterpreters.) The realisation that the sitting Taoiseach did not qualify for a tax clearance certificate from the Revenue (demanded of most of those undertaking state contracts) caused barely a ripple of concern in the party. Even when it was revealed that IR£30,000 from a Fianna Fáil constituency account was used to buy a house for Ahern's girlfriend Celia Larkin, no senior party figure could be found to express disquiet. Even the party's resident intellectual Martin Mansergh denounced condemnations of Ahern's behaviour as 'synthetic pseudo-ethical furores'. This defiance was bolstered by the knowledge that Ahern could get away with it. Politically, there was no price to pay: Ahern was re-elected as Taoiseach in 2007 even though he had admitted being on the take.

In many ways, the explanations of Ahern and of those who had given him money brought public life to a new low by openly appealing to a culture of cronyism that he seemed to regard simply as the way things were done. When pressed as to why he appointed people who gave him money to state boards, such as Aer Lingus, Dublin Port and Enterprise Ireland, Ahern stated on RTE television that 'I didn't appoint them because they gave me money, I appointed them because *they were my friends*'. This perfectly encapsulated the problem of what Brian Lenihan would later describe, in relation to the banking crisis, as the problem of Ireland being a small country 'with too many incestuous relationships'.

This, after all, was the point of the relationship between businessmen and politicians. There were certainly times when there was a direct exchange of money for favours – as in the case of Haughey in the 1980s making tax changes that conferred massive benefits on Dunnes Stores, whose boss, Ben Dunne, was one of his main benefactors. Mostly, though, it was all about being on the inside track, being in the know, getting your calls returned, being able to have that quiet word. It was also a kind of freemasonry – acquiring a reputation for being one of the lads (and it was all lads) conferred an aura of knowledge and authority that impressed one's peers.

In explaining why he gave Bertie Ahern money even though he barely knew him, one businessman, Barry English, encapsulated this attitude perfectly: 'I work in the construction industry and my clients are developers and the like and I don't think it does me any harm to be known as a friend of Bertie Ahern's.' On the other side of this exchange, Ahern's expression of gratitude to English was equally telling: 'He said, "Thanks very much and I'll sort you out."'

The other side of this warm glow of inclusion was the fear of exclusion. If membership of the circle gave you the sense that you were being 'sorted out' by the Minister for Finance (as Ahern was at the time of the dig-out by English and other businessmen), not being one of the lads made you wonder whether a rival was being sorted out ahead of you. In the RTE documentary *Bertie*, Ahern's money-man Des Richardson explained of the first dig-out in December 1993, when he raised IR£22,500 for his pal, that 'If I wanted to raise IR£100,000 for Bertie Ahern, I could have done that in one week'. He subsequently explained to the present writer what he meant by this statement. Richardson referred to a payment of IR£5,000 from Pádraic O'Connor of National City Brokers (a payment O'Connor maintained he intended for the party, not for Ahern personally): 'I could have raised IR£100,000 for Bertie in one week, and let me explain how. Pádraic O'Connor from NCB had given me IR£5,000 for Bertie. If I had gone to every stockbroker in Ireland and said "Pádraic O'Connor/NCB has given me IR£5,000 for Bertie Ahern, who was minister for finance at that time, so I would like you to do likewise", in my view, they would have been falling over themselves to do so, just to maintain a "perceived" level playing pitch for their company. It's all about perception.'

In the minds of those who were raising money for Fianna Fáil (and Richardson was the party's chief fundraiser), business people were not giving money because they wanted to support democracy but because they 'perceived' that otherwise their company would be playing on a pitch that was slanted against them. In many ways, it barely matters whether that perception was accurate or not. It served in itself to create both the fear of not being on the inside and the promise of being 'sorted out' if you were. It tilted relations between money and politics, business and the state away from the general public interest and towards a search for mutual benefits in which politicians got access to the money and business people got access to the politicians.

The beauty of this dependence on 'perception' is that it is unquantifiable, unaccountable and therefore limitless. A system in which everyone knows that bribes have to be paid in return for favourable treatment from the authorities is obviously sleazy. But one in which everyone is trying to size up who's in and who's out is more insidious and in some respects even more corrosive. Because it is fluid and unspoken, it is also unbounded. For those who see themselves as insiders, it generates a sense of being untouchable. And for those who see themselves as outsiders, it creates a sense of fear. They never feel they quite know what's going on. They believe there is a power that could, if it wished, do them harm. They learn to be cautious, watchful and discreet.

On both sides of this equation, there were dire consequences. For those on the inside, the sense of being untouchable fed what would become a hysterical hubris. For those who were making big money in banking and property, the belief, as Bertie Ahern put it in 2006, that 'the boom times are getting even more boomier' (and would continue to get even more boomier still) was a potent enough drug, creating its own delusions of invulnerability. But its effect was greatly enhanced by the idea of having a special relationship with power.

That relationship was ideological as well as financial. Besotted with the idea that the titans of free enterprise could do no wrong, Fianna Fáil politicians convinced themselves that their close alliance with the builders and developers was in fact a form of public service. The interests of the nation were those of the men who made the money and the men who made the money were those who gathered in the Fianna Fáil fundraising tent at the annual Galway races, a favourite meeting place for property developers, builders and party bigwigs. As Bertie Ahern told the *Irish Times* in 2004, 'If there are not the guys at the Galway races in the tent who are earning wealth, who are creating wealth, then I can't redistribute that.'

The reality that Ahern's governments made damn sure that the wealth of the guys in the tent was not redistributed anywhere does not mean that this statement was insincere. It perfectly encapsulated the mix of half-baked egalitarianism and crony capitalism that characterised Fianna Fáil's governing style. Ireland was one big tent, but that tent was full of developers, builders and other rich men making substantial donations to the party.

The sense of intimacy (or, in less attractive terms, incestuousness) that was epitomised in this relationship set the tone for a great deal else in Irish institutional and business culture. From banks run by board members who were directors of each other's companies to regulators and civil servants going to work for the companies they had been supervising, the ethics of the small world permeated Irish business. The problem was that Ireland was no longer a small world, but an extremely open, fast-growing global economy in which the stakes were getting ever higher.

On the other side of the equation, that of the outsiders, the consequences were less obvious but just as·lethal. If the insiders felt untouchable, the outsiders worried about laying a glove on them. The sense of impunity enjoyed by those within the circle was tangible and obvious. Especially if you were in the business of attempting to regulate, control or supervise the massively growing areas of the indigenous economy like banking and property, you had to take notice of the fact that some people belonged to a circle whose circumference was never quite defined.

The assumption that there were clear, unambiguous ethical and legal standards that could be upheld without fear or favour did not apply in an atmosphere where fear and favours were always in the air. Rules seemed to apply to some and not to others, and it was a matter of conjecture and surmise as why this should be so. The guesswork would have been foolishly incomplete if it did not include the question of political connections.

Above all, ethics became irrelevant. The lines between thievery and patriotism, between private advantage and the national interest, became impossibly blurred. And if you were a public servant who was supposed to be guarding those borders and ensuring that they were not crossed, you were patrolling a minefield.

3
Ethitical Banking

'For God's sake, whatever you do, don't rock the boat'
– Maurice O'Connell, governor of the Central Bank

It was rather apt that the Irish Central Bank literally could not spell the word 'ethical'. One of its inspection reports on a small Dublin merchant bank, Guinness and Mahon, which was running a huge tax scam for its clients, expressed the view that 'it is not, in our view, appropriate or ethitical [*sic*] for a bank to participate in, as distinct from advise on, tax avoidance schemes'. Stumbling over ethics was one of the bank's specialities. A central cause of the disaster that hit the Irish financial sector in 2008 was a culture, both of banking and of bank regulation, in which right and wrong were strange and elusive concepts.

For more than thirty years before the Irish banking system collapsed, it had been colluding, on a massive scale, with fraud, tax evasion and routine breaches of exchange control laws. Large sections of the Irish business class, from strong farmers to chairmen of blue chip companies, were hiding money in offshore accounts or claiming to be living outside the country when they were in fact making that money in shops, pubs, property deals and companies within its borders. While pre-Celtic Tiger Ireland was suffering from mass unemployment, mass emigration, a squeeze of vital services in health and education and a persistent crisis in its public finances, many of its most respectable citizens were simply absenting themselves from society. The banks were helping them to do so, and the authorities in turn were scrupulously ignoring what was going on.

The scale of the racket can be judged from the amount of tax that was eventually harvested after media investigations had prompted official inquiries. In all, the Revenue was eventually able to identify 34,000 people who had engaged in one or other of five major tax-dodging enterprises. By April 2009, it had recovered €2.5 billion from these individuals. To put this in perspective, €2.5 billion is almost a tenth of the entire Irish national debt in 1987. These people, of course, were simply those who were ultimately caught.

The important point about these scams, however, is that they were not secret conspiracies, so wickedly brilliant that even the best minds in the public service could not penetrate their dark purposes. The truth is that, in the case of two of the largest scams – the widespread evasion of Deposit Interest Retention Tax (DIRT), and the elite Ansbacher con, in which wealthy individuals salted money in the Cayman Islands to evade tax – both the Central Bank and its political master, the Department of Finance, had a damn good idea of what was going on. To understand the sickness at the heart of the Irish banking system it is necessary to grasp the extraordinary fact that the state authorities knew about widespread organised crime committed by financial institutions and their customers and did essentially nothing to stop it.

As the scandals unravelled in the late 1990s, the Central Bank, which regulated the system throughout most of the relevant period, would claim that its job was to make sure that the banks were solvent, and that issues like tax evasion were not really its business. It is worth noting that this claim was always patent nonsense. As the High Court inspectors who

investigated the Ansbacher con put it, 'from the very beginning of banking regulation the [Central] Bank was required
to have regard to qualitative factors. These factors included
the quality of the management of a bank and the nature of
the activities being carried on by a bank. Thus, whilst it has
been emphasised . . . that the Bank is not principally concerned with Revenue matters, the Bank was and is statutorily
obliged to concern itself with the proper regulation of banking. In this context, any evidence that a bank was facilitating
tax evasion was at all material times a matter of concern for
the Bank.' To put it simply, if evidence that bankers were
engaged in, or colluding with, financial crimes wasn't the
Central Bank's concern, it is hard to imagine what would be.

1 I'm Not There

Deposit Interest Retention Tax (DIRT) was introduced in
1986. It obliged banks to withhold tax at source from the
interest paid to borrowers and pass it directly on to the Revenue. Non-residents, however, could sign a form stating that
they did not ordinarily live in Ireland and therefore request-
ing that DIRT not be taken from their interest payments.

Ireland turned out to have an extraordinary number of
non-residents with accounts in its banks. Almost immediately on the introduction of DIRT, the number of absentee
depositors increased threefold. By the end of 1998, 17 per
cent of all Irish-held deposits (amounting to IR£7.6 billion)
was held by non-residents. The number of alleged expatriates
was staggering: Allied Irish Bank alone had 88,000 of them
in 217 branches – an average of over 400 per branch.

Given that the country had, at the time, almost no immigrant population, and that the figure excludes all of the financial institutions that actually dealt specifically or main-ly with non-residents, it was patently obvious that something was up. It was not hard to figure out what that something was: very large numbers of people were simply walking into their local branch, signing the forms, and claiming with a straight face to be resident outside the state. In many cases, these were people who must have been well known to bank staff. Equally, many of them were farmers, publicans, shop-keepers or small business owners tied to their towns and vil-lages, and the banks knew damn well that they could not possibly be living outside Ireland. But the flow of money was good for business: in one branch of National Irish Bank in Killarney, for example, the angry manager complained to his superior that he had lost more than IR£1 million in deposits after he was instructed not to open bogus accounts. But this was not a question of one particular bank behaving badly: 'the problem of DIRT evasion', as the Dáil Public Accounts Committee (PAC) put it in its report on the affair, 'was an industry-wide phenomenon'.

Every single one of these account holders committed an act of fraud by filling out a form claiming to be a non-resident. Yet, even though the forms were simple enough, many of them were not filled out correctly. As late as 1999, over a quarter of the relevant forms were not properly completed. As Mark Hely-Hutchinson of Bank of Ireland explained of a typical example of non-residents: 'Well, if he is a farmer, which means, by definition, he is a resident, part of his diffi-culty might be that he doesn't know quite which answers he ought to give to make sure that he evades the tax.'

Mostly, however, the banks didn't even bother about incomplete or incorrect forms. As the internal auditor of

Allied Irish Bank (AIB), Tony Spollen, put it, the 'feeling was that once the declarations were complete or once the declarations were there, and in some instances even if they weren't, that once the depositor said: "I am a non-resident", then I think that was almost taken as good enough.' As frauds go, this one was pathetically easy to pull off – it wasn't even necessary to lie properly.

Senior management in the banks knew that their branches were assisting in fraud, tax evasion and breaches of the exchange control laws. In AIB, for example, a senior executive, Henry O'Brien, wrote in an internal letter that sample audits in branches had shown that 'In general there is not a major problem in Dublin or the East Coast Area, but from West Cork to Donegal the position is bad in a large number of Branches' – meaning that it was clear at high levels within AIB that branches throughout the western half of the country were colluding in the fraud.

The second largest bank, Bank of Ireland, does seem to have adopted a policy of complying with the tax laws when DIRT was first introduced. In the first year of the tax, it lost IR£120 million in so-called 'non-resident' deposits, primarily because it was insisting on evidence that account holders were actually non-residents. Bank of Ireland quickly got the message and joined the other banks in facilitating their customers' crimes. When its chief executive, Mark Hely-Hutchinson, who suffered from the affliction of moral scruples, proposed to the Central Bank that there should be a common code of conduct among all the banks that would stop them undercutting each other's standards to get business, he received, as he recalled it, 'a very sort of warm, polite response, "What a pity these other people don't have the same ethics as you do." But the Central Bank simply didn't see it and it wasn't, within the legislation, within its function to police these things.' It says much about the ethical climate in Irish banking that a patently decent man like Hely-Hutchinson was left with little choice but to continue to oversee practices he clearly despised.

As we have seen, it was in fact a key part of the Central Bank's function to ensure that banks were behaving lawfully. The very existence of these bogus non-resident accounts, moreover, was itself a breach of the exchange control laws. The Central Bank, which was specifically charged with implementing those laws, as the PAC found, 'took no action'.

Even on an extremely conservative view of the role of the Central Bank – that it was there to ensure that the banks remained solvent – the fiddling of the DIRT tax should have been extremely alarming. In the case of AIB, the internal auditor, Tony Spollen, estimated in 1991 that the amount of money in bogus accounts was of the order of IR£300–400 million – which would mean that the unpaid tax was around IR£100 million. The chief executive of the bank, Gerry Scanlan, dismissed these calculations as 'infantile', but they were in fact a decent guesstimate. IR£100 million was, at the time, about the size of AIB's annual profits – the liability could in principle have pushed the country's biggest bank into the red.

This massive fraud was so obvious that even the authorities could not help noticing. The official files of the Department of Finance are seasoned with statements like 'half the non-resident accounts are thought to be bogus' and 'at least IR£1 billion of non-resident deposits are thought to be held by Irish residents'. By 1993, the Department's own internal estimates were that the amount of money in bogus accounts was IR£2 billion.

Why was nothing done? One reason is that the state saw

its job as supporting the banks rather than controlling them. The Public Accounts Committee, in its report on the scandal, concluded baldly that 'There was a particularly close and inappropriate relationship between banking and the state and its agencies. The evidence suggests that the state and its agencies were perhaps too mindful of the concerns of the banks, and too attentive to their pleas and lobbying.'

Thus, for example, when DIRT was being introduced, the Irish Bankers Federation lobbied the Department of Finance to ensure that the powers of the Revenue to look into the status of bogus accounts would be limited. The banking lobby was particularly concerned that the Revenue might inform foreign tax authorities about Irish accounts held by people claiming to be their citizens. It received an assurance from Maurice O'Connell, a senior Finance official who was later to become governor of the Central Bank, that 'there would be no "en bloc" disclosure'.

Beyond this tendency to see the interests of the banks as a paramount concern, however, there were broader assumptions at play. Deeply embedded within the state were two related beliefs. One – never openly articulated but clearly assumed at the level of unconscious instinct, and therefore especially potent – was that the rich in Ireland could not be expected to have any sense of social or patriotic responsibility. Misty-eyed nationalism may have come easily to the Irish high bourgeoisie, but the financial policy-makers knew better. They assumed that the Irish rich were similar to the elites of developing countries in Latin America or Africa. Given any level of pressure, they would evade their taxes and salt their money away offshore.

Secondly, the conclusion to be drawn from this was not the obvious one that the law would therefore have to be enforced with rigour and consistency. It was, rather, that the lawlessness of the rich would have to be indulged. Enforcement would become another art of avoidance, steering clear of anything that might scare them into hiding their money. Maurice O'Connell, then governor of the Central Bank, told the Comptroller and Auditor General that 'We were broadly aware of the fact that people were avoiding tax. And all this had to be corrected, this was wrong. Everybody agreed it was wrong. [But] for God's sake, whatever you do, don't rock the boat.'

If keeping the boat steady meant winking at widespread and flagrantly criminal tax evasion, then the winkers were serving 'the national interest'. Here, for example, is the general secretary of the Department of Finance from 1987 to 1994, Seán Cromien, explaining to the PAC why, in spite of knowing about the large-scale evasion of DIRT, he never recommended that the tax authorities be given more powers to deal with the problem:

CHAIRMAN: The question which you didn't answer, Mr Cromien, was – did you do anything, did you make any recommendations? If so, will you tell us briefly what they were?
MR CROMIEN: I realised that there was no point in recommending to Ministers that Revenue should be given these powers and if I were to do it, I think I would be worried myself that they would cause the outflows [of capital].
CHAIRMAN: So you made no proposal?
MR CROMIEN: I found it wasn't in the national interest to make proposals.

In this bizarre logic, the 'national interest' came to be identified with the interests of those who were fleecing the nation. The way to get the rich to pay their taxes was to make it easy for them to evade their taxes.

Given the close relationship between the Department of Finance and the Central Bank, it is unsurprising that these assumptions should have been held in common. Maurice O'Connell, who had discussed the banks' concerns about DIRT and disclosure in his role as a senior Department of Finance official, became the governor of the Central Bank. In that role, he oversaw a virtually complete failure to pursue the widespread criminality that was evident in the evasion of DIRT. This is how he justified that failure to the PAC:

> The Central Bank participated at various times in discussions about the taxation of interest on deposits and non-resident accounts. The Bank believed there was a problem regarding false statements on non-residents' status but it had no direct knowledge of the amounts that might have been involved, however, because the focus of its inspection is prudential and it does not embrace taxation . . . We had no way of quantifying it. We had no legislative authority to go in and quantify it. We were unhappy about it. We shared with the Department of Finance our views on this. We discussed ways and means . . . as to how we might find a solution.

Here is what the PAC concluded in this regard:

> There is nowhere in the evidence given at the hearings, or in the documents discovered to the [PAC], evidence supportive of the view that the Central Bank was engaged with deposit takers in working out the problem of bogus non-resident accounts. The evidence suggests that the

Bank saw itself as having no role in tackling the problem
. . . There was an insufficient concern with ethics and
supervision other than from the standpoint of a traditional and narrow concern with prudential supervision in the
Central Bank.

Throughout all of this, the banks themselves never got
around to discussing the ethics of what they were doing. The
boards of the banks, often made up of leading members of the
business community and of the legal and accountancy professions, made almost no effort to stop the institutions which
they ran from colluding with criminality. As the PAC report
put it, 'Boards of directors of financial institutions generally
betrayed an overly relaxed attitude towards discharging their
statutory and fiduciary duties in respect of the operation of
DIRT . . . Given the eminence of many of the members of the
boards . . . it is surprising that they did not bring a greater
weight to bear on the enforcing of ethical standards either
within their organisations or the banking sector generally.'

2 Cayman Ireland

The Ansbacher scam was a high-level, elite version of the
bogus non-resident accounts. It was established in 1971 by
the small Dublin merchant bank Guinness and Mahon
(G&M) and initially run as Guinness Mahon Cayman Trust.
After 1988, it became the responsibility of the Irish branch of
the Ansbacher group, and was known as Ansbacher (Cayman) Limited.

These changes in ownership had little impact – at all times
the operation was under the control of Des Traynor, even

after he ceased to run the bank itself in 1984. Traynor was not just a highly regarded financier and businessman (from 1987 until his death in 1994 he was chairman of one of Ireland's most successful companies, Cement Roadstone), he was also widely known as a close friend of Charles Haughey. (Traynor and Haughey had met in the early 1950s at the accountancy firm Haughey Boland.) He was also, in reality, the bagman for the voraciously corrupt Haughey, raising funds and managing them to support the Fianna Fáil rajah in the grand manner to which he believed his status as national hero entitled him.

Traynor's Ansbacher Cayman scam was simple in principle, if rather less so in practice. Essentially, members of Traynor's circle – the eventual Revenue haul would take €105 million from 137 people – would give him money, which he would deposit, through front companies, in the bank's Cayman Island accounts (and to a lesser extent in similar accounts in the Channel Islands). These deposits would be unrecorded in Ireland except on secret coded files held by Traynor (Haughey himself, for example, was S8 and S9). The same clients would then 'borrow' money from G&M in Dublin. The security for these 'borrowings' (the offshore funds) was not listed on G&M's accounts. The 'loans' were merely described as 'suitably secured' or 'adequately secured'.

The advantages of this arrangement were considerable. The clients had access in Dublin to money that was supposedly offshore. They could make lodgements and withdrawals through Traynor even though the money was stowed in a tax haven. And because of the system of so-called 'back-to-back loans' (essentially clients borrowing their own money), an asset was recorded for tax purposes as a debt. Instead of having large chunks of cash, the clients could pretend that they had in fact borrowed it. Herein lay the combined brazenness and ingenuity of the scheme. Instead of merely hiding the money from the tax authorities, Traynor's clients could actually claim tax relief on their 'borrowings'. There was a certain magnificence to the effrontery. It evokes the same admiration as a gangster who robs a bank and then claims compensation because his own account has been emptied.

As a licensed bank, G&M was subject to regular inspections by the Central Bank. The 1976 inspection was carried out by three inspectors, one of whom, Adrian Byrne, subsequently became the Central Bank's head of banking supervision, a position he still held in 2002. It seemed to these inspectors highly probable that G&M's offshore subsidiary in the Caymans was involved in tax fraud. The deposits it held, noted Byrne, were 'part of a scheme which was surrounded by a unique level of secrecy and which appeared to involve tax evasion'.

Yet, in reporting on this apparent fraud, the inspectors adopted the tone of a maiden aunt who has peered through a neighbour's window and inadvertently seen him indulging in a private and intimate pleasure. Metaphorically, they made their excuses and left. 'The bank', they noted, 'is in effect offering a special service which assists persons to transfer funds, on which tax has been avoided, to offshore tax havens. The possibility of the bank abusing its position as an authorised dealer in providing this service cannot be ignored. In view of the delicate nature of these matters we did not pursue the matter further . . .'

With an admirable fastidiousness, the inspectors broached the subject with the directors of Guinness and Mahon. The directors 'were initially reluctant to give information about the activities of these companies to the Central Bank because it [*sic*]

57

feared that the information might be conveyed to the Revenue authorities' – a concern that the inspectors clearly both understood and assuaged. They agreed that they would be shown documents relating to the deposits on condition that they would not note the names of the owners. Its inspectors having written that the bank's abuse of its licence 'cannot be ignored', the Central Bank proceeded effectively to do precisely that. Beyond a desultory communication to the effect that the Central Bank was 'somewhat concerned' and some inconclusive meetings with Des Traynor, nothing was done to stop what the inspectors strongly suspected to be a large-scale tax scam.

Even more helpfully, the Central Bank doctored its own internal files to minimise the nature of the Ansbacher fraud. In the report of the 1976 inspection, the phrase 'tax evasion' was later altered, by Byrne's superiors, to 'tax avoidance'. This was done again in relation to a document drawn up by Adrian Byrne two years later. A statement that 'the fact that the bank takes such extreme precautions to keep the existence of the deposits secret from the Revenue Commissioners indicates that the bank might well be a party to a tax evasion scheme' was altered to again replace 'evasion' with 'avoidance'. In evidence to the High Court inquiry into Ansbacher, Byrne referred to this complete change of meaning, in which unlawful evasion is redefined as lawful avoidance, as 'coding'. It might more accurately be called a deliberate act of unknowing by Byrne's superiors. If the Central Bank knew that Des Traynor was operating a sophisticated tax fraud, there would have to be consequences. The Central Bank 'knew' instead that Traynor was just a clever banker, lawfully working the system to suit his clients.

One reason for this tendency to call a crook a sheep-herding implement may have been the realisation that one of the

Central Bank's own directors was implicated in the Ansbacher fraud. At least by 1978, the Central Bank knew that one of those directors, Ken O'Reilly-Hyland, was one of Traynor's chosen few. At that stage, O'Reilly-Hyland, a Central Bank director from 1973 to 1983, had a 'loan' of IR£426,000 from Ansbacher Cayman. This knowledge, confirmed in the Central Bank's 1978 inspection, remained entirely inert and unofficial: 'There appears', noted the High Court inspectors, 'to be no documentary record within the Bank recording receipt or consideration of this information.' By 1988, O'Reilly-Hyland's Ansbacher 'loan' exceeded IR£1 million.

Since the early 1960s, Ken O'Reilly-Hyland had been a pivotal figure in the nexus of connections between business and politics in Ireland. He was one of the directors of Taca, the controversial Fianna Fáil fundraising organisation associated with the young and ambitious new generation of politicians whose most prominent figure was Charles Haughey. At the time that the Central Bank discovered his involvement in the Ansbacher Cayman scam, O'Reilly-Hyland was chairman of Taca's successor organisation, the so-called 'general election fundraising committee'. This was a secret body, not under the control of the party leader and not given to publishing accounts. It operated, not from party headquarters, but from the discreet privacy of Room 547 in the Burlington Hotel in Dublin. As chairman of this committee, O'Reilly-Hyland was involved not merely in obtaining large donations from wealthy business people, but in securing loans from some of the very banks the Central Bank was meant to supervise.

As well as being deeply embedded in Fianna Fáil's financial dealings, however, O'Reilly-Hyland was also part of a network of business connections among fellow holders of Ansbacher Cayman accounts, including the architect Sam

Stephenson, the solicitor who had acted for G&M in establishing its Cayman operations, Liam McGonigal (both fellow members of the Taca committee), and the auctioneer John Finnegan. Finnegan in turn was connected through the builders Brennan and McGowan to another powerful Fianna Fáil politician, Ray Burke. In 1984, Finnegan, jointly with Brennan and McGowan, made what a tribunal of inquiry subsequently found to be a 'corrupt payment' to Burke.

At the end of the 1970s and in the early 1980s, O'Reilly-Hyland was caught up in tensions between the secretary of his Fianna Fáil fundraising committee, Des Hanafin, and the new party leader, Charles Haughey. Haughey wanted direct control over the committee, and Hanafin, suspecting his motives, resisted. Haughey was particularly anxious to get hold of the committee's so-called Black Book, a top-secret list of donors. Infuriated by Hanafin's resistance, Haughey decided to disband the committee. A stand-off ensued until, shortly after Haughey was re-elected as Taoiseach in 1982, he summoned the committee members to his Georgian mansion at Kinsealy and got them to sign a document ordering Hanafin to hand over the secret fund-raising accounts into his own control.

O'Reilly-Hyland told the Moriarty tribunal that at the time of his appointment to the board of the Central Bank in 1973, he informed the then minister for finance, George Colley, that he had an offshore trust in the Cayman Islands. That this was no barrier to a role as guarantor of the integrity of the country's banking system was itself eloquent testimony to the prevailing standards in public life. O'Reilly-Hyland cannot but have placed those in the bank who were trying to uphold higher standards in an excruciatingly difficult position. In evidence to the Moriarty tribunal, O'Reilly-Hyland stated that it had not at any stage been brought to his attention by the governor or by any other official within the Central Bank that his dealings with Traynor's scheme had been discovered by its inspectors. This reluctance to raise the issue suggests that it was regarded as a painful embarrassment.

The then deputy general manager of the Central Bank, Timothy O'Grady-Walshe, told the Moriarty tribunal that he could not remember seeing documentation referring to O'Reilly-Hyland's dealings with Traynor, but he 'thought it probable' that he had done so. He 'imagined that it should have raised questions within the Central Bank. As to whether it was taken further than himself, he stated that he did not know, but was confident that it was highly probable that he had spoken to the Governor and the General Manager about the matter.' However, the Central Bank governor of the time, Charles Murray, told the tribunal that it was possible that he had been told about O'Reilly-Hyland but had then forgotten the information. If he were informed, he said, it would have been up to him to decide whether or not to inform the other members of the Board, but he doubted very much whether he would have informed them.

There is no evidence that knowledge of O'Reilly-Hyland's involvement in the Ansbacher tax evasion scam had a direct bearing on the Central Bank's supine approach to this web of financial crime. Some of those at high levels in the bank, however, knew two things. One was that one of their own directors was deeply involved in both the scam itself and in Fianna Fáil. The other was that Des Traynor, who was running the Ansbacher fraud, was close to the new party leader, Charles Haughey. In a supervisory culture that was already remarkably deferential, such knowledge was hardly likely to encourage bold scrutiny.

The then governor Charles Murray suggested at the

Moriarty tribunal that if Adrian Byrne's view was that tax evasion had been involved, or if the record in that regard had been changed, he should have pressed the matter by bringing it to a more senior member of staff. Adrian Byrne himself explained to the Moriarty tribunal that the Central Bank's approach to G&M was shaped by two factors. One was a narrow concern with keeping G&M in business. The Central Bank, he said, had two options: it could have revoked the bank's licence, or it could have demanded the resignation of certain directors. He said that either course of action would most likely have led to the bank's collapse and depositors would have lost money. The Central Bank's priority was to stop this happening. At the same, time, the regulators held Traynor in high esteem. When Traynor promised them after a second inspection in 1978 that he would begin to wind down the Cayman scheme, they believed him. 'We thought', said Byrne, 'that he would work his way out of this.'

During 1979, before Haughey took over as party leader and Taoiseach in December, the Central Bank began to express more forceful concerns to Des Traynor, pointing out rather plaintively that the Ansbacher scheme was 'not in the national interest'. In theory, these apparent warning shots should have become louder after Haughey's election. The arrival of the Boss into power was the signal for a massive growth in the scale of the Ansbacher scam. In April 1979, the deposits stood at just under IR£5 million. Three years later, they had reached almost IR£27 million. By then, the Cayman operation, initially a sideshow, had become larger than its parent company.

This happened in spite of the Central Bank's own weak-kneed compromise with Traynor. Instead of closing down his operation and calling in the police, it merely extracted from him an informal agreement that the Ansbacher racket would be kept at its current levels. Even when it discovered in 1982 that the Ansbacher deposits were in fact increasing significantly, the Bank did nothing.

As the Moriarty tribunal concluded, 'despite increases in the level of lending, references to substantial new loans being backed by deposits, and other matters which might reasonably have induced the Central Bank to wonder as to . . . the value of Mr Traynor's assurances, few if any further inquiries were made. Indeed it seems that the interest on the part of the Central Bank in the off-shore activities that had been foremost in its concerns when reporting in 1978 thereafter dwindled and largely ground to a halt.'

This may or may not have been connected to something else the Central Bank discovered in 1982. In December of that year its exchange controls division received a formal request from a man who wanted to take out a foreign currency loan to the tune of UK£350,000. The request, on behalf of Abbeyville Stud, clearly stated that the lending bank would be 'Guinness Mahon Cayman Trust Ltd, PO box 887, Grand Cayman, British West Indies' and that, as security, the title deeds to the stud farm would be lodged with Guinness Mahon Cayman Trust Limited. The signature on the letter was that of Charles J. Haughey. It was delivered personally by Des Traynor to the general manager of the Central Bank. Approval was issued the following day, a response time that may say more about the source of the request than about the bank's efficiency.

It is striking that the Central Bank's scrutiny of G&M, never very acute, became far less inquisitive after Haughey – who was using the bank to hide much of his wealth – came to power. At a review meeting in April 1981, there was, as the

High Court inspectors' report puts it, 'some passing reference to particular loans with a Cayman connection' but 'no further discussion of the overall nature of this banking activity or of its taxation implications'. The Central Bank conducted further examinations of G&M in 1986, 1988 and 1992 and failed every time to blow the whistle on what was now a large-scale criminal conspiracy involving the country's most senior politician.

The regulators of the financial system never got to the bottom of Traynor's system, and never worked out the precise mechanism of his 'back-to-back' loans. But this was in part because the Central Bank failed to use its powers to compel the full disclosure of Traynor's records. In hindsight, Adrian Byrne acknowledged, as the Moriarty report put it, 'that he and his colleagues should probably have pressed Mr Traynor harder on access to documents, but nonetheless this was a substantial person in the banking community whom they had trusted; whilst there were strong suspicions, and some like himself had believed that evasion was involved, it was another thing to prove this. Put by Tribunal Counsel that all that was needed was good reason [to demand the full records], and that this did exist, Mr Byrne responded that he did not disagree and that this was an option, but they had taken the course of accepting that the loans in question would be run down . . . Although there were some isolated indications of reductions in loans, Mr Byrne agreed that there had been no reduction overall, and that some increases in loans had been very marked, and this should have produced more action on the part of the Central Bank. He was in no doubt that untruthful information had been forthcoming from Mr Traynor. The matter should not have been dropped after the priority that had been given to it in the earlier inspections.'

A last opportunity to launch a full investigation into Traynor's scheme arose in 1988 when a neophyte inspector, Terry Donovan, was sent to accompany two more senior colleagues on their visit to G&M. He quickly cottoned on to the very strange nature of G&M's business and raised his concerns, both with the bank itself and later with his superiors at the Central Bank. The details of what happened thereafter are contested, but Adrian Byrne told the Moriarty tribunal that 'whatever Mr Donovan may have said or not said, concern was not triggered within the Central Bank'.

What is completely clear is that, as the Moriarty report put it, for the Central Bank as a whole, 'the serious unfinished business of the back-to-back loans and Mr Traynor's undertakings was permitted to be ignored or forgotten'. Equally clear is that, apart from the detailed mechanics of the scheme's operation (such as the secret codes), the Central Bank had the strongest suspicions that Des Traynor was operating a large-scale scam. As the Moriarty tribunal concluded, 'the Central Bank inspectors were made aware of the essential features of the back-to-back loan arrangements in question, whereby Irish residents were enabled to earn interest on offshore deposits free of tax.' Had it acted on what it knew, as Moriarty pointed out, it would not merely have put a stop to Traynor's swindle, 'it would in all probability have accelerated the rate and level of response on the part of regulatory authorities generally to abuses within Irish banking that were not unique to Guinness & Mahon.' It might, in other words, have changed the broader culture of Irish banking.

Instead, the Central Bank didn't just keep its knowledge of the Ansbacher fraud to itself, it continued to do so even after the scam became public in 1996. In a letter written to the Minister for Finance, Charlie McCreevy, in November 1997, and subsequently read into the Dáil record by McCreevy, the governor of the Central Bank, Maurice O'Connell, stated that 'There is no record that the Bank had discovered the system for operating the Ansbacher accounts during its inspections and review meetings. Prior to publication of the [McCracken] tribunal report, the Central Bank had no knowledge of the existence of the "Ansbacher Deposits" referred to during the tribunal hearing or of the role played by G&M [Guinness and Mahon] in the management of those deposits.'

After it emerged that the Central Bank in fact had extensive knowledge of the Ansbacher deposits, McCreevy read out another letter from O'Connell in the Dáil on 30 March 2000. O'Connell claimed that his earlier letter meant that 'the Central Bank had no knowledge of the system of numbered offshore deposit accounts known as the "Ansbacher deposits". These appear to have been deliberately concealed and were maintained outside the normal books and records of G&M.' His claim of ignorance had referred only to the actual method of operating the accounts (which the bank did not in fact know about). The apparently definitive statement that 'the Central Bank had no knowledge of the existence of the "Ansbacher Deposits"' – a claim that was, on the face of it, patently false – did not mean what it might seem to mean. McCreevy, moreover, threw his own weight behind this exercise in semantic escapology: 'in respect of the issues which arose in the course of on-site inspections by the Central Bank in 1976 and 1978 concerning back to back loans secured by offshore deposits, it would seem that these activities formed part of the G&M accounting system and from the Governor's letter of 9 February 2000 it would appear that the term "Ansbacher accounts" or "Ansbacher deposits", as used in the Governor's letter dated 11 November 1997, was not intended to cover these accounts. My advice is that it would not be appropriate to enter into discussion on this distinction as this is a matter for the [Moriarty] tribunal.'

By the time of the High Court inquiry into Ansbacher in 2001, Adrian Byrne was declaring himself 'very betrayed by a lot of people in Guinness and Mahon, particularly Mr Traynor'. There is no doubt that the complex mechanisms through which the fraud was operated were unknown to him and that he was lied to by Des Traynor, who had assured him that the scam would be wound down over time. It is clear that he was both skilled enough to detect the stench of corruption from the Guinness and Mahon accounts as early as 1976 and had the moral sensibility to know criminal tax evasion when he saw it. Byrne was a highly capable and moral public servant.

The fact remains, however, that Byrne, as he became more senior at the Central Bank, never managed to take any effective action against what was in effect a multi-million-pound criminal conspiracy. That a decent and intelligent public servant could fail in this way is indicative of the culture of banking regulation in Ireland: if the good guys were so weak, it is hard to imagine that the banks had anything to fear from the time-servers. Byrne himself became a key figure in banking regulation during the Celtic Tiger years, firstly as the Central Bank's head of banking supervision and then, until 2005, as the personal adviser to the chief executive of the Irish Financial Services Regulatory Authority. Even after his retirement from that role, he remained the confidant and golfing partner of the chief regulator, Pat Neary.

The DIRT and Ansbacher scandals had immediate implications for the way the subsequent economic boom unfolded and imploded. In the first place, their outcomes copper-fastened a sense of impunity. Tens of thousands of people, including a large slice of the business elite, defrauded the Exchequer of hundreds of millions of pounds. The consequences ought to have been profound. Instead, they were simply non-existent. Although two huge criminal conspiracies had been uncovered, there were no prosecutions. The answer to the question asked by Michael McDowell in 1994, in relation to corruption in the beef industry – 'Will any of these people hang their Armani jackets on the back of a cell door in Mountjoy [jail in Dublin]?' – was still a resounding 'No'.

Not only was there no legal accountability, there was no managerial responsibility either. There was no clear-out of senior bank management. The blue chip accountancy firms whose audits had somehow missed the fact that their clients were colluding in large-scale fraud remained in business. The banking culture in which everyone raced towards the bottom of the ethical barrel for fear of losing business to a more unscrupulous rival remained entirely intact.

There was not even a loss of prestige for those grand figures at the top of Irish banking who had failed to take the DIRT scandal seriously. One example was Peter Sutherland, who was chairman of Allied Irish Bank when it emerged internally that the bank held hundreds of millions of pounds in deposit in bogus accounts. Sutherland was, among other things, a former pillar of the state's legal system, as attorney general from 1982 to 1984. Yet, as Sutherland told the PAC inquiry, he did not really see the DIRT fraud as a matter for him: 'The issue of non-resident accounts and DIRT was an issue which was essentially one for management. Management, as I understand it, believed that the issue was under control . . .' Sutherland passed the whole unpleasant business to the bank's audit committee, headed by the man who would succeed him as AIB chairman in 1993, Jim Culliton. Though Sutherland was presumably unaware of the fact, Culliton was the holder of an Ansbacher Cayman account. Yet this passivity on Sutherland's part did him no harm at all. He continued to be a hugely admired figure in Irish business, the man most Irish bankers aspired to be.

More broadly, Irish banking did nothing to create a collective ethic, a set of common standards that would ensure that nothing like the DIRT and Ansbacher scandals could happen again. Even at the time of the DIRT inquiry, the chief executive of one major financial institution, Roy Douglas of Irish Life and Permanent, could not bring himself to regard the Ansbacher scam as anything out of the ordinary:

> MR DOUGLAS: It's clear from the documentation that there were certain depositors in this jurisdiction who had, effectively, placed money on deposit with Ansbacher Cayman, and that is one set of relationships. For its part then, Ansbacher Cayman had placed the money on deposit with Guinness & Mahon and that's a quite different and unconnected – in effect, as I understand the law – relationship.
> DEPUTY RABBITTE: Is it the same money?
> MR DOUGLAS: Well, in effect, legally it's not the same money . . . there was an amount equating with the amount that these Irish residents had placed on deposit . . . with Guinness & Mahon from Ansbacher Cayman.
> DEPUTY RABBITTE: So, you'd forgive the man in the street for believing that it was the same money?
> MR DOUGLAS: I think that obviously there was a clear – it would appear from the documentation – connection.
> DEPUTY RABBITTE: . . . do you professionally consider, Mr Douglas, that this is a fairly extraordinary legal construct?

MR DOUGLAS: To be frank, Deputy, I don't. I think that is the simple straightforward set of relationships that exist between a depositor and a bank.

As the PAC put it, 'the contention by Mr Roy Douglas of Irish Life and Permanent (now owners of Guinness & Mahon) that the Ansbacher device "is the simple straightforward set of relationships that exist between a depositor and a bank" is astonishing and lacking in any credibility'. The problem was that, within the world of Irish banking, it was less astonishing than it seemed to ordinary mortals outside that world and was, in fact, perfectly normal.

Irish banking created for itself a cosy narrative of the scandals: they had been unfortunate, they had been dealt with and we had all moved on. Seán FitzPatrick, then chief executive of Anglo Irish Bank, and as it later turned out, a master himself of ethical banking, put it best in 2005: 'My own industry of banking had the issue of DIRT to deal with and, as an industry, our actions were clearly wrong in the past. We failed to deal with the issues appropriately; we were wrong, and we have paid the price for our misjudgement. However, what's important in this context is that the issue of DIRT was capable of being dealt with under existing legislation and under existing procedures. We did not need any new [regulatory] powers.'

This was self-serving nonsense. The DIRT scandal was not a misjudgement, it was a criminal conspiracy. The bankers had not 'paid the price', they were left serenely alone. And the issue was not 'dealt with' under existing procedures, unless dealing with it meant some handy manoeuvres with a brush and a carpet. But FitzPatrick's view was that of both the regulators and the bankers: nothing had really happened.

It was hardly surprising therefore that there was no

change in the regulatory culture. The Central Bank's apparent denial in 1997 that it had known about the Ansbacher scam kept pressure off it at a crucial period when regulatory reform was being considered. Supervision of the banks was still shaped by the mindsets that allowed the scandals of the 1970s, 1980s and 1990s to unfold without interference. Those scandals had shown the regulators to be at best too timid to act on their moral principles and at worst actually complicit in the anarchy of the bankers. There ought to have been a revolution in the whole approach to the supervision of a rapidly growing financial services industry. Instead of transformation, there was almost complete continuity.

Two particularly toxic elements remained in place. One was an extremely conservative notion of the purpose of banking supervision. The apparatchiks of the Central Bank and of its successor, IFSRA, never shook off the belief that regulation was overwhelmingly prudential, which is to say that it should concern itself in a narrow way with the fiscal stability of the banks. So long as a bank seemed to have sufficient assets to meet its obligations, everything else was of minor importance. They never grasped the idea that ethics also mattered, that the ability of managers to adhere to basic moral and legal standards was a good test of the sustainability of their institutions. This habit of seeing decent and responsible behaviour as, at best, a side-issue was to have fatal consequences in the years of turbo-charged growth.

The other disastrous habit of mind was less easily identified but, if anything, even more lethal. What is clear from the Central Bank's fitful and pitiful attempts to deal with the Ansbacher Cayman scam is that politics mattered. It is not that any of the Central Bank inspectors or their superiors were themselves part of a political conspiracy or cover-up.

There is nothing to suggest that any of them were motivated by anything other than a desire to do their jobs in difficult circumstances. But those circumstances were immensely complicated by the knowledge that officials were dealing, not just with bankers over whom they held regulatory power, but with bankers connected to politicians who in turn held power over the regulators.

There is, in the Ansbacher case, an unmistakable correlation between political power (in effect, Fianna Fáil) and regulation, with the Central Bank's level of scrutiny rapidly diminishing after Charles Haughey came to power. What is important about this correlation for subsequent events is that it was entirely unspoken. There is absolutely no evidence of direct political interference in the workings of the Central Bank. There are no threatening phone calls and no Fianna Fáil moles on the bank's staff. Things are much subtler, and much more insidious, than that. In the very small and overlapping worlds of Irish banking, business, politics and public service, people knew who Des Traynor was and for whom he worked. They knew that there was a system of networks and connections, with the ruler of the country at its centre. This knowledge did not disappear after the scandals emerged in public. It was reinforced by the utter impunity from legal consequences of those who had engaged in flagrant fraud. Inchoate, instinctive and perhaps even unconscious, that awareness was all the more powerful because it did not require those who held it to do anything. On the contrary, it required them to do precisely nothing. And so, when it came to regulation the Irish tricolour became an idiosyncratic set of traffic lights: orange for 'hang on a minute', white for 'oh dear, my mind's gone blank' and green for go.

4

Our Own Gentry

'Let me tell you about the very rich.
They are different from you and me.'
– Scott Fitzgerald

In his *Begrudger's Guide to Irish Politics*, Breandán Ó hEithir
told the story of a priest talking to a small farmer in Cork in
the late nineteenth century about the imminent blessings of
Home Rule. We would, the priest assured the sceptical
farmer, have our own parliament, our own police, our own
church, our own flag and our own gentry. The farmer nod-
ded respectfully and silently. As he moved away, he growled,
in a mordant undertone, 'We will in our arse have our own
gentry.'

In the unbearably hot August of 2003, the feared French
riot police, the CRS, moved in on the small town of Gallardon, south of Paris. The main street and several others were
blocked off and the local shops had to close. The operation
was a response, not to the presence of a terrorist cell or the
discovery of chemical weapons, but to an Irish celebrity wedding. Two members of the Irish gentry, Georgina Ahern,
daughter of Bertie, and Nicky Byrne, a member of the boyband Westlife, were uniting their dynasties in nuptial bliss.
The twelfth-century Church of St Peter and St Paul had been
chosen for its picturesque qualities, not least for the impression it would make on the readers of *Hello* magazine, which
had paid €1 million for the rights to the event.

Even though the shopkeepers grumbled about the loss of

business, the citizens of Gallardon seemed happy enough to tolerate the general inconvenience. In their culturally impoverished condition, none of them had heard of Westlife, and many assumed that the famous Irish pop-star groom must be Bono. The evident opulence of the preparations fed rumours that David Beckham and Prince Charles were going to turn up. In compensation for the heavy security presence, they expected a more elaborate version of the town's usual Saturday ritual. As one resident explained to Lara Marlowe of the *Irish Times*, 'There are weddings here every Saturday. It livens the place up. People come out to see the bride's dress, and they always applaud.'

When the citizenry went down to their church, however, they got a nasty surprise. Not only were the riot police keeping them from getting too close, but the entire entrance to the church was concealed by a large white tent, like a giant wedding veil hiding its demure face. Cars with curtains on their windows drove into the tent, so that bride, groom and guests could be spared the greedy gaze of the populace. Brawny security men in morning suits zipped and unzipped the entrance to the tent.

Watching this non-spectacle, the locals quickly realised that those who had taken over their town and disrupted their lives were not even going to give them a cheery wave in return. As one lady put it, the people had been treated 'like imbeciles'. 'We gave them our little village. We were happy to do it. And they didn't even have the decency to say hello.'

And something stirred, some memory perhaps that France had once had an aristocracy of its own and had replaced it with the idea of a republic. As Marlowe reported, 'the onlookers' anger exploded. There were cries of "C'est dégueulasse" (It's disgusting) and rude comments about the bride and groom. Each time the veiling operation occurred – on arrival and post-wedding departure for the silver van carrying the bridesmaids and the black Mercedes which brought the Taoiseach and his daughter – the catcalls grew louder.' The French, at least, remembered how to jeer the gentry.

There had been a kind of dress rehearsal for Georgina and Nicky's nuptials eighteen months previously, when both were guests at the wedding of another Westlife member, Bryan McFadden, to Kerry Katona, an event that was similarly purchased by *Hello*. This time, the wedding was in the village church of Rathfeigh in County Westmeath. Access to parts of the village and to the church were similarly blocked off, even after the end of the wedding, and *Hello*'s investment was likewise protected by burly security guards and blacked-out cars. The Irish taxpayer paid for fifteen gardai to be on duty to keep citizens at a distance, and gratefully provided a pair of Garda motorcycle outriders to flank the bride's wedding car. As the newly-weds drove away from the ceremony in their blue Rolls-Royce, the gardai ran alongside the car to shield its occupants from prying eyes and preserve *Hello*'s *droit de seigneur*. But whereas the French villagers had rebelled and jeered, the Irish crowds behaved with impeccable peasant propriety. 'Loud cheers', reported the papers, 'greeted the guests as they were ferried in a convoy of tinted-window minibuses and Mercedes saloons from Slane Castle.' Ireland had its own new gentry and no memory of the guillotine to cut through the celebrity culture with a sharp edge of republican self-respect.

In some respects, the most puzzling aspect of what happened in Ireland in the Celtic Tiger years is the tolerance of an increasingly confident and educated populace for the emergence of what was, in all but the external trappings of title and accent, a new aristocracy. This was a much more substantial new elite than that generated by the outrageous fortunes of manufactured pop. But it tapped into a grander version of the same cult of celebrity. And it would prove to be, in its own way, almost as insecure as the instant fame of reality TV shows and assembly-line bands.

The concentration of the new wealth created by the boom could hardly have been more extreme. Excluding the considerable value of its residential property, the personal wealth of the top 1 per cent of the Irish population grew by €75 billion between 1995 and 2006. Bank of Ireland Private Banking estimated in 2007 that, including private residential property, the top 1 per cent of the population held 20 per cent, the top 2 per cent held 30 per cent and the top 5 per cent held 40 per cent of the wealth. Even this picture was somewhat distorted by the puffed-up book values of middle-class houses. If residential property was left out of the equation, the top 1 per cent held 34 per cent of the wealth.

Even at the apex of this pyramid, moreover, there was an extreme concentration of wealth. Of the 33,000 millionaires (again not counting house values), the vast bulk had less than €5 million. Three thousand had between €5 million and €30 million. Just 330 had more than €30 million. In the last three years of the boom (2004 to 2007) alone, the richest 450 people in Ireland added €41 billion to their combined personal wealth.

Yet, somehow, Irish people went on believing that they lived in a relatively classless society.

There were a number of reasons for this, chief among them the old Irish association of 'upper class' with the Protestant Ascendancy, meaning that a Catholic aristocracy was a contradiction in terms. But another crucial factor was the way the rise of the new elite in Ireland coincided with the global culture of celebrity.

Bertie Ahern himself was the key to all of this. His brilliance lay in his capacity to connect the old power structures of Fianna Fáil and the native business elite to the new global celebrity culture. He did this through the creation of 'Bertie', a character who tapped into the tabloid celebrity world while keeping hold of a very old-fashioned Irish political machinery.

Celebrity culture thrives on two qualities. One is false intimacy – the belief that a famous person is known to us in the way our friends, family and neighbours might be. The other is blankness – the celebrity is a screen onto which we can project whatever feelings, thoughts or desires we choose at any given time. 'Bertie' superbly encapsulated both of these qualities.

In politics, blankness might seem to be a weakness, but the Bertie persona turned it into a strength. Except under extreme pressure, Ahern could hide real feelings like anger, contempt or greed under a warm blanket of mundane amiability. He could be a friend to everyone, even his enemies – knowing, of course, that the politician who was attacking him today might want to do a deal tomorrow, or that the voter who was venting spleen on the doorstep might just change her mind in the polling booth. He could be a socialist with a trade union leader, a neo-liberal with a business leader. He could share with a property developer his contempt for tree-hugging environmentalists and with the Green Party a passion for sustainable development. This adaptability and opportunism, this talent for absorbing all sorts of forces within himself, may have had their source in a kind of emptiness, but they functioned splendidly in the shifting landscape of boomtime Ireland. He had no hard core of moral passion to weigh him down as he modulated from friend of the rampant rich to every worker's pal. This allowed him to embody the evasiveness of a society that was in many minds about its own reality.

Even the impression of a certain kind of stupidity – his famous ability to mangle even the flattest of cliches ('smoke and daggers', 'upset the apple tart') often made George Bush sound like Abraham Lincoln – could enhance the power of blankness. Bertie underplayed his own keen intelligence, sometimes deliberately resorting to gibberish, not caring if it made him look obtuse and inarticulate. He downgraded the grandeur of his office by being infinitely available to ceremonially open pubs, hairdressers, supermarkets or packets of crisps. He deliberately gave the impression that he cared more about Manchester United or the Dublin Gaelic football team than about health policy or poverty. It allowed people to get used to the idea that he was not in fact willing to engage in any serious discussion about the direction of Irish society, and even to the notion that such matters were tediously irrelevant.

The blankness gave him more than the ability to remain, for all the apparent permanence of his power, a moving target. The famous Teflon surface that allowed him to deflect obvious questions about, for instance, his relationship with Charles Haughey, in which he was both the Boss's favourite protégé and entirely ignorant of his master's misdeeds, was also a screen onto which people could project an image they liked. It allowed for the other great celebrity quality – the false intimacy that turned Bertie into the embodiment of familiarity, the ordinary Joe with ordinary desires who just happened to be running the country.

Like all celebrities, he dished up selected slices of his real, private life. It ought to have been a problem in a country that still had a very high level of Catholic belief that, uniquely among international leaders, Bertie was a still-married man who not only lived with his girlfriend but made her the official first lady who accompanied him on state visits and hosted heads of state and government. There ought to have been some sympathy for the poor, conservative Archbishop of Dublin who not only had the Taoiseach's partner's beauty salon opposite the entrance to his palace, advertising Brazilian waxes, but who actually received an invitation to an official state reception in her name. But in fact the drama of Bertie's complex love life was perfectly consonant with the pop-culture worlds in which his broader family, with its bestselling popular novelist daughter Cecelia and his boyband hero son-in-law, was firmly embedded.

'Bertie', in other words, was the image, not of a ruthless politician whose mentor was flagrantly corrupt, but of a character in a long-running soap opera. Such characters are meant to be people like us, except that an absurd number of dramatic things happen to them. Their marriages break down, they have complicated, drawn-out love affairs, their children marry pop stars and have twins, or become famous novelists overnight. Their careers follow strange paths, with unlikely and sometimes downright incredible twists. But they themselves remain solid, reliable, familiar. The things that happen to them are functions not of their character, but of the plot.

This is the way Bertie Ahern was seen, and it was the reason for his legendary invulnerability to scandal. When he signed blank cheques for Charlie Haughey, as he did for long periods in the 1980s when he was treasurer of Fianna Fáil, it wasn't something he did but something that was done to him, as the innocent victim of an older man's wiles. When he brought Ray Burke back into cabinet in spite of specific allegations that he was on the take, it wasn't a conscious decision, just an accidental turn in a complicated story of which he knew nothing. When he got money from businessmen, it was something they did to him, an event beyond his control. He was as surprised as any of us would be if our friends suddenly gave us envelopes containing thousands of pounds while we were having a pint in the local. And when he had to explain that money as news of his 'dig-outs' became public, he did so by shifting it back onto the soap opera territory of private life, in which he could no more help what happened than Ken Barlow in *Coronation Street* could help leaving Deirdre for Denise and then Denise for Deirdre.

The importance of Ahern's brilliant manipulation of celebrity and soap-opera norms was not confined to his own outstanding success in winning elections. It was not even limited to the way this greedy, money-grubbing man with wads of cash in his safe managed to make pretty much everyone believe that he was an ordinary fella, who was interested in money only to the extent that he needed a roof over his head, a few pints and a subscription to Sky Sports. It did more than any of that – it provided cover for the emergence under Ahern of a new aristocracy. It harnessed one kind of elitism (celebrity culture) to the interests of another – the operation of a governing class that (often quite literally) floated above the reality of Irish society. 'Bertie' mediated perfectly between the existence of an aristocratic elite on the one hand and the public belief, on the other, that there were no class distinctions in Ireland.

To call the new super-rich elite an aristocracy is not as

whimsical as the absence of blue blood or old money may make it sound. Nor is it simply a reflection of its desire for country mansions and racehorses, or even of its preference for the helicopter view of Ireland. (The property developer Seán Mulryan and his wife, for example, flew in and out of their gloriously restored manor and stud at Ardenode in his-and-hers Sikorskys.) What made the elite an aristocracy was precisely its successful insistence on the privilege that defined the French aristocracy before the revolution: exemption from taxes.

One of the effects of the sense of victimhood in which much of Ireland's billionaire class wrapped itself (see Chapter 5) was the absence of any sense of social responsibility. The patriotic urge was more than adequately fulfilled by taking over old Ascendancy estates or buying up half of London's West End. It did not need to be expressed in sentimental gestures like paying one's taxes. This was a *noblesse* untroubled by *oblige*.

For much of the early period of the Irish boom, sophisticated tax avoidance was entirely unnecessary. Good old-fashioned tax evasion was perfectly adequate and almost entirely risk-free. The Revenue, indeed, began the boom period by writing off, in 1996, €1.8 billion in unpaid taxes – none of it, it is safe to say, owed by ordinary PAYE workers – as 'uncollectable'.

In 2002, the Comptroller and Auditor General gave the public a unique glimpse into the tax dealings of a highly successful, but unfortunately unnamed, property developer. He (a safe assumption is that it is a 'he') was in business since 1970 but, presumably not being a man to rush things, didn't make a tax return until 1988. Not one – for eighteen years. He was tempted out of the shadows by a tax amnesty brought in by Fianna Fáil in that year. For eighteen years of property development, he paid a grand total of €79,000 in tax. This was 'considered inadequate' by the Revenue but it never got round to asking for more money.

Having made his grand gesture, the developer promptly disappeared again. A demand from the Revenue for €450,000 in corporation tax was returned to sender. The Revenue let it lie on the basis that 'neither of the two directors could be contacted', and in 2000 this tax was written off. Remarkably, this Invisible Man was involved, throughout the 1990s, in thirty-five major property developments, including 'several major industrial estates, office blocks, apartment blocks, townhouse schemes and a shopping centre, with recent [in 2002] developments valued at over €125m'.

The idea that one of the country's larger property developers couldn't be contacted with a tax demand may seem implausible, but the story actually became even more fantastical. Of the developer's thirty-five companies that were registered for corporation tax (they paid a measly total of €250,000 between them), twenty-five were registered for VAT and none was registered for PAYE or PRSI. In the paper world of officialdom, their employees could not pay tax because they did not exist. One company that was recorded in the official records as 'dormant' somehow managed to construct with this staff of ghosts 'two townhouse developments and an apartment block in the early 1990s which sold for €10m'.

When one Revenue demand for €34,000 in VAT arrears was returned to sender, a tax official contacted the developer's registered address and was informed that the company had transferred to another address, and that the whereabouts of the directors were unknown. At the second address, the official was told that the company no longer existed. Again, the VAT arrears were simply written off.

In an ordinarily dysfunctional society, the property developer who could build thirty-five major developments without paying tax and avoid prosecution would be content to bask quietly in the knowledge that he could do whatever he liked. Our hero, however, had the panache of the true aristocrat. When he sold his own house for €3.9 million, he was not considered to have any liability for residential property tax because 'his declared income was below the income threshold'. There was a genuine elegance about the circularity of this brazenness – he didn't pay tax because he had declared hardly any of his income; he didn't have to pay tax because the income he declared was so low. The V-sign was flicked with a nerveless insouciance that commands applause.

With the relatively brief upsurge of public disquiet that followed various tribunal revelations – Haughey's voracity, Burke's backhanders, Lowry's evasions – and the DIRT inquiry in the early 2000s, this kind of open taunting of the tax authorities became rather less advisable. What happened, however, was that the Fianna Fáil/Progressive Democrats government offered an alternative. The alternative was not, as might naively be imagined, that people who were making millions would pay their taxes in the same way as those who were making mere thousands. That would imply that these categories of people were somehow to be regarded as equals. Instead, illegal (though unpunished) tax evasion would be turned into perfectly legal tax avoidance.

Some of this strategy consisted in either cutting taxes or deliberately leaving loopholes in tax laws. The wealthy, and especially property developers, benefited enormously from one of Charlie McCreevy's first moves as Minister for Finance – cutting the rate of capital gains tax from 40 per cent to 20 per cent. Developers also gained enormously from a loophole in stamp duty legislation, which allowed them to purchase or transfer, tax-free, shares in companies owning land rather than technically buying the land itself. (The whole transaction was treated as a transfer of company ownership rather than of property, thus avoiding the bulk of the tax.) This created a bonanza for the super-rich: the developer Bernard McNamara saved €36 million on a single deal (the purchase of the Glass Bottle Company site in Dublin's docklands). Over 40 per cent of big property deals exploited this loophole, but the government refused to close it.

For complete aristocratic immunity from taxation, however, it was necessary for the government to construct an even more abject scheme. Most democracies have problems with what the Irish called 'tax exiles' (making them sound like melancholy and martyred refugees) and the Americans, who take tax more seriously, rightly call 'tax fugitives'. Ireland was one of the very few countries to go out of its way to make it as easy as possible to be a tax fugitive. In essence, Fianna Fáil and the PDs deliberately concocted a ruse whereby it was possible, if you had your own jet, to live in Ireland and abroad at the same time. As if Ireland did not have enough bogus non-residents, they summoned into existence a whole new (and entirely lawful) host of spectral beings whose whereabouts were more a matter of hovering than of being.

Again, the gift was bestowed by Charlie McCreevy. The existing situation was that, in order to claim not to be resident in Ireland for tax purposes, it was necessary to spend more than half the year (183 days) abroad. This did not suit the super-rich, so McCreevy played Fairy Godmother and invented the 'Cinderella clause'. A day, it turned out, was not a day if you left the country by midnight. It was possible to work in Ireland all day and still technically not be in Ireland. So long as the golden carriage of the Lear jet was in the air at the witching hour, you were in no danger of returning to the plebeian ashes and rags of nasty taxes.

Not that anyone was likely to be checking anyway. Figures uncovered by the *Sunday Tribune* in July 2009 showed that just nine individuals (0.15 per cent of the total number of tax fugitives) were audited by the Revenue to ensure that they were operating within the rules. It was hardly surprising that the numbers of rich people accepting McCreevy's gift rose steadily. While McCreevy was in office, the numbers were never revealed. From 2005 onwards, they became public: in 2005, there were 3,050 people claiming non-residency for tax purposes. In 2006, there were 3,996. In 2007, there were 5,142. And in 2008, there were 5,803.

These figures included 440 'high net worth' individuals – defined by the Revenue as those with net assets of more than €50 million. This was a very large slice of the Irish business elite. Most of the best-known figures amongst the super-rich were tax-resident elsewhere: Dermot Desmond in Gibraltar, John Magnier, J. P. McManus and Hugh McKeown in Geneva, Michael Smurfit in Monaco. (Tony O'Reilly has not been tax-resident in Ireland since he left Ireland to work for Heinz in the 1960s.) These men all retained major business interests in Ireland: Desmond, for example, remained active in fields ranging from health insurance to telecommunications to banking, and was even offered the chairmanship of Aer Lingus in 2008. McKeown remains chairman of the largest private company in Ireland, the food distributors Musgrave. Smurfit was chairman of the biggest Irish-based multinational company, the packaging conglomerate Smurfit Kappa, until 2007.

The starkest case was that of the telecoms and media billionaire Denis O'Brien. O'Brien built the bulk of his fortune from the acquisition of a public asset – the state's second mobile phone licence – in circumstances subsequently investigated by the Moriarty tribunal. He then sold on the company that held the licence, Esat, to British Telecom for €2.4 billion. Just before he did so, however, he changed his tax residency to Portugal, saving himself capital gains tax of €55 million. He continued to live in his mansion on Raglan Road in Dublin, which the Revenue tried to insist was his 'principal residence'. He established that he could not in fact live there because the house did not have a kitchen. He also maintained a large house in Thomastown, County Kilkenny, and continued to run his large Irish media businesses.

There was, though, a further refinement on this abstract game of absence and presence. Some very rich men began to wonder whether it was actually necessary to spend any time outside Ireland at all. Why not send the wife instead? Gerry McCaughey, who had stood unsuccessfully for the PDs in the 2002 general election, owned and ran Ireland's largest timber-framed house construction company, Century Homes. He sold it for €74 million in 2005 – his share was €31 million. Behind this transaction, however, there was a touch of magic from the accountants KPMG. They suggested that McCaughey and three other main shareholders should sell their shares to their wives, who would in turn sell them on to the real purchaser. The wives, meanwhile, would go to live in Italy to avoid capital gains tax. All that was required to stop the peasants from getting their hands on any of McCaughey's gains was a languid 183-day holiday on the Riviera.

This ruse was perfectly legal, but it also perfectly illustrated the almost pathological aversion to paying tax among the Irish rich. Capital gains tax, at 20 per cent, was low. In McCaughey's case, it would have left him with €25 million instead of €31 million. How much difference would this have made to his family's way of life? But the money itself was not really the point. As McCaughey explained when the ruse was revealed, 'People do everything they can to reduce their tax liability.' Not to engage in tax avoidance was to be a non-person. In some societies, and for 'maverick' Irish billionaires like Ryanair's Michael O'Leary, paying substantial taxes might be a source of pride. For the Irish elite, it was a source of shame. To be in on the latest wizard scheme was to be 'one of us'. It was the definitive mark of separation between the First Estate of unimaginable wealth and the Third Estate of PAYE toilers who didn't get to play the game.

It would be wrong to conclude, however, that the game itself was particularly difficult or that it could only be played with smart-alec schemes. This was a game whose rules were fixed to ensure that there could only be one winner. The government, which was supposed to be the referee, was relentlessly biased towards tax-phobic citizens. It introduced, and kept in place, a dazzling variety of tax reliefs. In 2004, the Revenue Commissioners estimated that these reliefs had an annual cost of €8.4 billion – nearly a quarter of the entire annual tax take at the time. This huge expenditure was so poorly policed, and so sketchily analysed in terms of the relationship between the costs and the supposed benefits, that the Revenue literally could not say, in the case of forty-four different schemes, how many people were claiming and how much money they were getting. The reliefs, of course, were overwhelmingly of benefit to the better-off.

The result was that, even leaving aside the top layer of the wealthy elite that was paying no tax at all in Ireland, the minor aristocracy enjoyed the privilege of paying tax at far lower rates than those that pertained to the rest of the country. The findings of a Revenue study of the 400 top earners (defined, it is important to remember, by their declared income rather than their actual wealth) in 2002 were stark. Six had an effective tax rate of zero – they had quite lawfully managed to pay no tax at all. Forty-three paid less than 5 per cent. Seventy-nine paid tax at less than 15 per cent. Conversely, just 83 paid more than 40 per cent, and none paid more than 45 per cent. To put this in perspective, the top tax rate for PAYE workers in the same year was 42 per cent.

Even when these reliefs were eventually limited in 2006, the impact on high earners was still relatively minimal. In that year, 439 individuals declaring over €250,000 each were able to claim €288 million in tax reliefs – an average of €650,000 each. For the 214 people in a Revenue study declaring over €500,000 in income each, three-quarters had an effective tax rate of between 15 and 20 per cent, and the rest paid between 20 and 25 per cent. Not one of them paid anything like the 41 per cent rate that then applied to middle-class incomes. Scott Fitzgerald began his 1926 short story 'The Rich Boy' with the words 'Let me tell you about the very rich. They are different from you and me.' Beneath its surface of classless bonhomie, Irish society in the boom years was underpinned by this dictum.

The government's response to figures like these unconsciously betrayed the belief that the rich elite did in fact constitute an aristocracy. Aristocrats are not taxed – they are bountiful. The government's chief ideologue, Mary Harney, responding in 2004 to questions about the ability of the rich to pay little or no tax, specifically ruled out any attempt to make them cough up on the same basis as everybody else. They might, however, feel like throwing some coins from their balconies: 'I would like to see perhaps in Ireland, on a voluntary basis, a greater culture of some of the wealth that is acquired going back to the state, not necessarily through taxes or through legislation but perhaps through endowments, through foundations.' There were, in other words, quite explicitly two classes of citizens: those at the bottom for whom taxation was compulsory and those at the top for whom it was voluntary.

Instead of seeking to end these distinctions, government politicians began to behave as if they were themselves part of the aristocracy. There was a sense that since, in their own eyes, they had done so much to create the boom, they ought to live like its heroes. It was therefore proper that they should be paid very large salaries. A *Financial Times* survey in March 2009, after the Taoiseach Brian Cowen had taken a 10 per cent pay cut, still found him to be almost at the top of the tree among world leaders. Dmitri Medvedev's salary was €67,000; Gordon Brown's was €199,000; Angela Merkel's was €228,000; Nicolas Sarkozy's was €240,000; Cowen's was €257,000 and Barack Obama's was €292,000. Even this somewhat understated what Irish leaders thought they were worth during the boom years. In 2007, Bertie Ahern proposed paying himself €310,000 a year, which would have made him the best-paid politician in the democratic world, had public opinion not forced a deferment of his salary increase.

This sense of entitlement to the high life was reflected in

the lavish conduct of senior politicians. Many ministers began to ape the ostentation of the class with which they identified. Even though they had high-end state cars and chauffeurs, they insisted on travelling like property developers, in helicopters and private jets. Sharing the motorways with ordinary citizens was beneath them – often quite literally. Between January 2007 and June 2009 alone, ministers used government jets or fixed-wing planes (a Lear jet 45, a Gulfstream IV, a Beech Super King Air and a Casa) and Air Corps helicopters 144 times for internal flights within Ireland. Mary Harney, for example, took twenty-four flights in that period, flying to exotic destinations like Galway, Cork, Kerry and Shannon. Harney had form: in December 2001, she used an official fisheries surveillance aircraft, part-funded by the EU, to fly to Leitrim to cut the ribbon for an off-licence store for a barrister friend of hers.

Abroad, Irish ministers travelled like sultans on tour. On one infamous trip to Florida, paid for by the state training agency Fás, Harney and her party took the government jet at a cost of €80,000. The taxpayer forked out $410 for hair treatments at their lavish hotel. The Arts, Sports and Tourism minister John O'Donoghue, his wife and his private secretary ran up a hotel bill of €5,834 in Venice. At the Cannes film festival, he stayed in the €990-a-night Hotel Montfleu and spent almost €10,000 on hiring a chauffeur-driven limousine. Another limo during a trip to the UK for St Patrick's Day came to €8,843.

In purely financial terms, this lavishness was of little importance, but as a statement of the way government politicians saw themselves, it mattered a great deal. It revealed the film that was running inside their heads, a glamorous, sun-kissed international epic in which they moved through a world of speed and ease, of drivers and flunkies, fine wines and gourmet dinners, in which money was of no consequence because it was infinitely available. It placed them, when they were not in the grubby world of constituency politics, in an insulated, air-conditioned universe, floating above the clogged-up, stressed-out, often squalid physical realities of life in boomtime Ireland.

This fantasy of celebrity glamour didn't just draw politicians into the mental universe of the super-rich. It separated them from the other side of aristocracy – poverty. The image of Ireland, as they lived it out with their high salaries and lavish expenses, was seriously out of synch with the reality.

One problem caused by the speed of the boom was a tendency to exaggerate just how rich Irish people really were. Because growth rates were so high, and because the general improvement in prosperity was so spectacular, Irish people in general felt rich. This feeling was bolstered by the figures showing GDP per capita rocketing above that of many other European countries, including the old master, Britain. But these figures were deceptive, both because GDP, which is simply an annual index of wealth-production, does not give an accurate reflection of things like accumulated wealth and quality of life, and because, in Ireland's case, it is significantly inflated by the financial juggling of transnational corporations with an interest in boosting profits in low-tax Ireland.

Thus, GDP per capita undoubtedly ranked Ireland as one of the wealthiest nations in one of the wealthiest parts of the world, the EU. But GNP per capita, which excludes the money that transnational corporations are sending home and is thus a more accurate measure of real national income, placed Ireland just slightly above the average for the fifteen member states of the old EU. So Irish people as a whole were not in fact all that rich. Even using the exaggerated measure of per capita GDP, average wealth per head was pretty similar to, for example, North Yorkshire or Oregon. If Ireland actually were, as Mary Harney and others liked to fantasise, a US state, it would have been the thirty-fifth richest, a little wealthier than traditionally underdeveloped Arkansas but poorer than Rhode Island, Nebraska or Georgia, and less than two-thirds as wealthy as New York.

When Bertie Ahern proposed to pay himself an increase of €38,000 a year, it was striking that this increase alone was greater than the total salaries of 1.5 million Irish workers. Three-quarters of the workforce, in other words, was on €38,000 a year or less – a very modest salary in a country with an extremely high cost of living, high levels of mortgage debt and social services. People paid through the nose for facilities like childcare that were free or heavily subsidised in other European countries. It is also striking that, certainly by late 2007, there was an obvious disjunction between the constant propaganda that told these workers that 'we' were rich and their own experiences. In a Bank of Ireland Life survey of people in full-time employment earning more than €30,000 a year, 70 per cent agreed with the description of Ireland as a 'wealthy country'. But 79 per cent also agreed with the statement that most Irish people were not really wealthy but rather were 'obsessed with the trappings of wealth'. And 76 per cent agreed with the statement that 'it's all about keeping up with the Joneses'. Ireland was rich, its people were not, and the gap between one reality and the other was filled by attempts to acquire the outward trappings of a wealth you did not really have.

Even for those in decent jobs who were clearly benefiting from the boom, the levels of debt required to service mortgages and run cars, combined with inflation rates that were much higher than the rest of Europe, were not conducive to feelings of economic security. In a Guinness/Amarach survey published in March 2002, when debt levels were nothing like what they would become by 2008, a massive 44 per cent of people agreed with the statement: 'I worry sometimes about how much money I have borrowed and whether I'll be able to pay it back.'

Below this broad mass of people who were doing reasonably well but anxious about debt there was a persistent level of squalor. Some of this was physical: primary school children in the largest classes in the EU, many in abysmally ramshackle, overcrowded and unsanitary buildings; hospital waiting areas so filthy and overcrowded that the regular comparisons with 'Third World' conditions were understandable exaggerations.

But the underlying squalor was social. The greatest shame of the boom years was the abject failure to get rid of consistent poverty. That it was possible to do this with the unprecedented resources at the state's command was acknowledged even by Fianna Fáil. In its manifesto for the 2002 general election, written with the experience of five years of government and presumably in the knowledge of what could be done even within the framework of Celtic Tiger orthodoxy, it made a bold pledge: 'For the next five years we are setting the historic target of effectively ending consistent poverty in our country, with a minimum target of reducing it to below two per cent.'

The best evidence of the failure to reach even this minimum target was the Fianna Fáil manifesto for the 2007 general election. It made no reference to the target at all, not even to repeat the promise. It stated merely that 'The achievements of the last 10 years confirm that we have the possibility of becoming one of the few countries in the world to effectively eliminate consistent poverty.' There was no target, no commitment, merely a bizarrely vague reminder of the 'possibility' that a country with the resources that Ireland had acquired could ensure that no one lived large parts of their life in poverty.

The reason for this complete shift in tone was obvious: the government had not ended consistent poverty or even reached its 'minimum' standard of 2 per cent. In 2007, at the height of the boom and after a decade and a half of almost uninterrupted growth, the level was two and a half times the minimum target. For children (7.5 per cent in consistent poverty), the picture was even uglier.

Beyond those living in poverty for long periods, the numbers defined as being 'at risk of poverty' also remained high. Eighteen per cent of the population was in this category in 2007 (compared to 10 per cent in the best-performing EU countries) – and 40 per cent of these people were children. With the collapse of the economy, rapidly rising unemployment and sharp cuts in public spending, these figures will certainly rise over the coming years.

The government failed so miserably to achieve its goals on poverty because it no longer actually believed in the republican concept of equality. With no sense of irony at all, it was the Minister for Equality, Michael McDowell, who told the *Irish Catholic* that 'A dynamic liberal economy like ours demands flexibility and inequality in some respects to function.' It was such inequality 'which provides incentives'. 'Driven to a complete extreme, the current rights culture and equality notion would create a feudal society.' The bizarre logic of this sentence perhaps betrayed the strain of excising equality from republicanism, which McDowell always claimed as his political philosophy. It was not the deliberate fostering of an unaccountable, untaxed super-rich elite that was in danger of creating a feudal Ireland, but the looming threat of the 'culture of rights' and the notion of equality as it stalked the Celtic Tiger to its lair. McDowell's view of the medieval world seems to have been shaped by the scene in *Monty Python and the Holy Grail* when peasants scrabbling in the muck declare themselves an 'anarcho-syndicalist commune'. The threat of revolutionary feudalists seizing power in Ireland was not unreal, and indeed it had already come to pass, but not quite in the way that McDowell's Pythonesque world-view seemed to imagine.

McDowell's leader, Mary Harney, helpfully glossed his comments for tabloid-reading dummies who might be confused by such convoluted thinking: 'It's like a football team: Some make premier division and others aren't so good, unfortunately.' If Ireland had both a Manchester United class of pampered and idolised superstars and a Drogheda United class of slow-witted cloggers, this had nothing to do with politics or power, but was simply the working out of genetic and temperamental differences: 'everybody is not the same, people have different skills, different capacity, different IQs, different strengths.' (Oddly, this apparent support for raw meritocracy did not prevent the government from protecting inherited wealth by abolishing estate duties and cutting inheritance tax.) The typical right-wing confusion of sameness and equality barely concealed a profound belief that inequality was the proper order of things. Genetic differences had simply expressed themselves in the fact that some people had lots of money and paid no tax and some people had very little money and paid lots of tax. This being so, the existence of a 'free' elite at the top and a slough of poverty at the bottom was simply inevitable. It was Social Darwinism and not crony capitalism that had decreed that the likes of the Bailey brothers should sit on top of the Irish evolutionary tree. That this might be a rather disappointing outcome to all those millennia of human development did not dampen the PDs' enthusiasm for the doctrine.

This was not just a minority PD view. Fianna Fáil, for all its republican posturing and occasional genuflections towards egalitarian ideals, held it too. Defending McDowell's remarks, Fianna Fáil minister Willie O'Dea said that 'If there's inequality of wealth in a society it gives people who aspire to better themselves the incentive to gain more wealth.' Inequality, by implication, was essential to the functioning of the economy. It was the red meat that fed the Celtic Tiger.

The social consequences of this new doctrine that inequality is good were obvious in the persistence poverty amid plenty. But the world-view which it expressed also fed directly into the economic catastrophe that was about to befall Ireland. It justified the notion of an elite that operated at a higher level than those who lacked their betters' IQs, skills and capacities could ever really comprehend. It encouraged politicians, who ought to have maintained a social and intellectual distance from that elite, to ape its ways and share its fantasies. It fed the egos of developers and the bankers who lent them larger and larger amounts of cash. Already high on self-delusion and a sense of invulnerability, the last thing most of them needed was a further boost to their egos. The Irish already had their own gentry. They didn't need them to start thinking they were kings.

5

The New Feudalism

'Just pucker up your lips and blow'
– Lauren Bacall,
economic adviser to the Irish government, 1997–2007

Paddy Kelly didn't have a Rolls-Royce. He had, as he corrected his interviewer, Eamon Dunphy, on RTE Radio at the end
of November 2008, 'several' Rolls-Royces. He didn't have a
house on Shrewsbury Road, where, perhaps because it was
the most expensive property on the Irish version of *Monopoly,* all the developers wanted to live. He had two houses on
Shrewsbury Road. He hadn't yet gone bust – that would take
another few months – and the 'hundreds of millions' of euros
he confessed to owing the banks were, he said, 'no great bur-
den' to him. But he was, nonetheless, one of the oppressed,
the heir to a legacy of great suffering and injustice whose
every triumph was a blow struck for history's victims.

Kelly liked to remind interviewers that his great-grandfather
and namesake had been evicted in the late nineteenth century
from his tenant farm in Abbeyleix and imprisoned for putting
up a poster on behalf of the Land League, which fought a long
and bitter struggle against the dominant land-owning elite. In
that radio dialogue in November 2008, as the men who had
led Ireland's astonishing property boom were entering the last
days of their golden age, Kelly recalled a phrase used by the
Fianna Fáil minister Kevin Boland in 1970. Denouncing those
who were standing in the way of the demolition of Georgian
Dublin and its classically proportioned streets and squares,

Boland called them 'a consortium of belted earls and their ladies and left-wing intellectuals'. The red-baiting and anti-intellectualism were there as ornamentation to the main theme: the new, brash Fianna Fáil developers were not crass money-men but the vanguard of the national revolution.

Property development was the new armed struggle, the war of independence by other means. Where Paddy Kelly's great-grandfather and his generation had taken on the landowning aristocracy with boycotts and rent strikes, and the next generation had burned down their big houses, now the people's struggle against the aristocrats was best conducted by building lucrative office blocks and densely profitable housing estates on the sites of their former townhouses and mansions. This wasn't greed, it was patriotism.

Paddy Kelly talked about his feeling of historic triumph when he was building houses on what was once the great Ascendancy estate of Castletown in County Kildare: 'It was time the Irish went through the front gate. I always remember Kevin Boland talking about the belted earls . . . We, the ordinary Irish, had to have a say as well.' He went on to talk of his great-grandfather and of his belief that his family had had its land confiscated in the Plantation of the seventeenth century: 'All that suffering in a sense is all part of what we are.'

This sense of historic vengeance suffused the mentality of the elite class of property speculators and developers who often came from humble, rural Catholic backgrounds and who rose sufficiently high to accumulate up to €90 billion of bad debts to Irish banks which the even humbler Irish taxpayer had to take on.

They derived a particular pleasure from parading themselves at archetypically British upper-crust events like the Royal Ascot racing festival, and at buying historically resonant English buildings. It was not accidental that Seán Dunne imagined his would-be redeveloped Ballsbridge as Ireland's answer to Knightsbridge. When the artificial 'island of England' off the coast of Dubai – aptly enough, built on sand – was sold in 2008, it was predictable that it would be bought by Irish developers who outbid British investors. The pleasure of owning England was worth the extra money.

When a syndicate led by the Irish developer Derek Quinlan fought off a Saudi oil sheikh, Prince Al-Waleed bin Talal, to buy the Savoy hotel in London (along with Claridge's and the Connaught), one of Quinlan's employees had the Irish tricolour flown from the roof, like the Russians taking the Reichstag. 'I cried', Quinlan recalled. 'My poor father, who was in the Irish army, would have loved to have seen this.'

When Pat Doherty's Harcourt Developments bought the old Conservative Party headquarters in Smith Square in February 2007, one of his directors, Mike Murphy, admitted that 'There is a kind of little buzz about it' and could not resist joking that the Tories themselves were not included in the purchase price. The tones were suave and sometimes sentimental. But if you listened hard, you could hear, unspoken but implied, the famous (and surely apocryphal) reply of a republican activist asked in the early twentieth century by an English reporter what the aims of Sinn Féin were: 'Vingince, bejasus!'

Yet only rarely did the thought seem to strike any of those who were constructing great fortunes in property that they were themselves the new landed aristocracy. That thought does seem to have crept uninvited into Seán Dunne's brain as he expounded on one of the favourite subjects of the new elite: the carping of the bitter little people. 'Jealousy and begrudgery', he moaned to the *New York Times* in January 2009, 'are still alive and well in Ireland, and whoever eradicates them should be prime minister for life. It's part of the Irish psyche and it is the result of 800 years of being controlled by other people, of watching everything the master or landlord is doing.'

The implications of Dunne's comment – that he and his cohorts were the landlords and masters being watched by the jealous peasants – were almost certainly unintended, but they were not untruthful. Leaving aside the ironies of those who saw themselves as representatives of an oppressed peasantry becoming the equivalents of the landlords who had oppressed their ancestors, the resonances of the nineteenth century were real. It was not just that boomtime Ireland retained a pre-industrial obsession with property as its preferred form of wealth, but that property in its rawest form – land – was at the heart of the strangely distorted economy that emerged from the late 1990s onwards.

On the surface, the story of the Irish boom was a tale of post-modern globalisation. It was about the miracle of a society that never had a proper industrial revolution and that suffered as a consequence from underdevelopment and all its attendant ills. This absence of old industry suddenly became an advantage in the high-tech, post-industrial, globalised economy of the 1990s. Without the leaden legacy of dying steel, coal, engineering or car manufacturing industries, Ireland could go straight from the almost pre-modern to the post-modern, skipping ahead into the bright, supercharged, ultra-connected future.

This story was not entirely unreal, but there was also another, parallel, narrative. It was barely modern, let alone post-

modern. As Kelly's harking back to his great-grandfather's suf-
ferings suggested, it was a weird unfolding in the globalised
twenty-first century of an intensely local nineteenth-century
psychodrama. Alongside the microchip manufacturers and
financial wheeler-dealers, the software engineers and concoc-
ters of wonder drugs, there was a rough, primitive struggle
for the control of land. Except that this time, the descendants
of the indigenous underclass were the ones on horseback and
it was the new urban and suburban workforce that was paying to keep them there. And there was no Land League to
fight the new Ascendancy.

If the control of land is left out of the equation, the sheer
scale of the Irish property bubble is impossible to fathom. In
most of the developed world, house prices generally rose
sharply throughout the 1990s and the early years of the
twenty-first century, but the Irish boom was certainly the
loudest in Europe, if not in the world. Between 1985 and
2006, prices in Finland and Italy rose by 50 per cent, in
France by 75 per cent, in the UK by 140 per cent and in Ireland by almost 250 per cent. Even these figures understate
the mind-boggling scale of the rise in Ireland during the peak
years of its property pandemic. Between 1994 and 2006, the
average second-hand house price in Dublin increased from
€82,772 to €512,461 – a rise of 519 per cent. If you'd spent
€1 million buying houses in Dublin in 1994, and sold them
twelve years later, you'd have made almost €4.2 million
profit without lifting a finger.

There were some good reasons for house prices to increase
in Ireland over this period. The population was rising, there
were more people in their twenties and thirties looking to
buy houses, and there were fewer people living in each
household. Rising levels of employment and prosperity made

it possible for more people to aspire to home ownership. The Irish obsession with having a secure home (rooted in a history of eviction and displacement) meant that the desire to own one's own house remained stronger than in other countries: 87 per cent of Irish households own their own homes, compared to an EU average of 61 per cent. The high cost of living in Ireland, combined with relatively high wages and burgeoning demand, meant that inflation in the construction sector was especially high.

In these circumstances, house prices were always going to go a little crazy in the Celtic Tiger years. The problem was that they didn't go crazy – they went stark, staring mad. This was an era in which, in the interests of full disclosure, estate agents ought to have foamed at the mouth and bitten their customers' legs.

The size of the bubble bore no relation to the rational factors that could have been expected to inflate it. The average price of a new house in the country as a whole in 1994 was €73,000. Michael Punch and P. J. Drudy worked out that if that price rose in line with the consumer price index, it would have reached €109,000 in 2007. If it rose in line with average earnings, it would have cost €124,000. If it followed the trend in runaway building-cost inflation, the price would be €132,000.

The actual price in 2007? €323,000.

In other words, new house prices increased over four times faster than house-building costs, five times average industrial earnings and more than seven times faster than the consumer price index. The cost of houses was so grossly inflated beyond what was happening in the rest of the economy that it made the Michelin Man look like Twiggy. The result in real terms was that mortgages became very, very expensive. At the height of the madness in early 2007, the average working couple in Dublin, buying a first home, was paying a mortgage of €1,741 a month – a third of its net income.

The main reason for this was the price of building land, which in turn was heavily influenced by what the Oireachtas All-Party Committee on the Constitution referred to as the fact that 'certain landowners had accumulated large land-banks at the outskirts of urban areas which they then released in dribs and drabs in order to manipulate the market and artificially to maintain high land prices'. Essentially, a small number of very wealthy land speculators was able to shape the market in such a way as to ensure that the cost of buying the land it stood on made up a larger and larger proportion of the cost of a house.

The practice of building up large private land-banks went back to the 1960s. Paddy Kelly, for example, began to build his land-banks around Dublin in the early 1970s. In 1973, the *Irish Times* reported that 'Mr Paddy Kelly of Woodland Homes has built continuity into his mini-estate operation by buying up a substantial "land bank" in the Dublin region. More of these parcels are in the three to ten acre bracket, although he has also bought larger holdings.' In 1981, he bought 80 acres of land in Clondalkin, giving him a very large stake in the development of the city on its western fringes.

Especially in the areas around Dublin, a tiny number of speculators and developers could control the supply of building land. In Fingal county – the area of North Dublin where most of the growth took place in the boom years – it was shown that just twenty-five individuals or companies owned 50 per cent of the building land in 2003. With this kind of power, the landowners were able to push up the prices they got from builders. Before the boom, land made up about 10 to 15 per cent of the cost of a house. At the height of the boom, it made up a breathtaking 40 to 50 per cent. Given the huge absolute rise in house prices, this generated vast profits for those who controlled the land. In 2003, Jerome Casey of the *Building Industry Bulletin* reckoned that the difference between the old, normal percentage of the price accounted for by land costs and the new, boomtime figures translated into €6.6 billion in extra profit. In other words, in one year alone, the small oligopoly of development landowners made €6.6 billion by controlling the market. Every cent of that was squeezed out of the poor saps who were buying the houses.

This massive inflation in the cost of building land had further costs for the average citizen. The country's infrastructure was seriously underdeveloped as the boom got under way and there was a need for very large-scale investment in roads and public transport. But the land on which to build this infrastructure now had to be purchased in a hyper-inflated market. Thus, land acquisition costs for the LUAS light rail project in Dublin were around €100 million – at one point in 2003, its developer, the Rail Procurement Agency, was paying €6 million per acre. Even for road-building, where most of the land in question was rural and agricultural and was not zoned for development, the public ended up paying through the nose. Merely widening a 14-kilometre stretch of one motorway, between Dublin and Portlaoise, in 2003 cost the taxpayer over €70 million – just to buy the land. The National Development Plan's estimate of €7 billion for its programme of road building and upgrading more than doubled to €15.8 billion. During the boom years, farmers and others made €11 billion from selling land, most of it to the state.

Even the cost of farmland with no official development status was pushed upwards, as Ireland returned to being an almost feudal state in which the ownership of land itself conferred untold wealth. Michael McDowell might have noticed this, since he spent €30 million of taxpayers' money buying a farm in North Dublin as the site for a new prison, but he persisted in believing that the feudalist threat came from those who were harping on about inequality. By 2007, Irish farm land values were the highest in Europe, at €66,000 per hectare – an incredible price in a country with plenty of arable land and a relatively sparse population. It was ten times the value of similar land in Scotland and six times more than the same fields would be worth in England. In May 2008, €13.5 million was paid for a 450-acre farm in Warrenstown, County Meath – one of the highest prices ever paid for agricultural land anywhere in the world.

There was no relationship at all between the astronomical price of farm land and the amount of money that could be made from actual farming. What was driving the increase was a mixture of speculators buying up land for potential development and farmers enriched from sales for public infrastructure projects looking to replace the fields they had sold.

The primal nature of this land-hunger is clear from the way Irish investors started to buy up farms in Scotland and England. According to the estate agents Savills HOK, 22 per cent of queries about Scottish farms on its books came from Ireland. In 2007, almost half of all British farm land sold to foreign buyers was bought by Irish purchasers.

How could this unsustainable frenzy have been allowed to

go on? One of the keys to understanding what happened in the Irish housing market is what didn't happen. For that, we have to go all the way back to 1973, and a document with the uninviting title *Report of the Committee on the Price of Building Land*. This committee was established in 1971 as a response to the anarchic explosion of badly planned housing during the previous Irish boom of the 1960s. It was not exactly a revolutionary cabal. It was chaired by Mr Justice Kenny of the High Court (hence it is usually called the Kenny report), and consisted of two representatives of the Department of Local Government (later called the Department of the Environment), with one each from the Department of the Taoiseach, the Revenue Commissioners and the Valuation Office. It would be hard to find a more sober body of deliberators outside of a working breakfast for imams in Mecca.

The committee's task was to find a method of 'ensuring that all or a substantial part of the increase in the value of land attributable to the decisions and operations of public authorities . . . shall be secured for the benefit of the community'. Or to put it in less sententious terms, to stop landowners from getting windfall profits just because the local authorities zoned their agricultural fields for development and serviced them with sewage, roads and water. You didn't have to be a socialist, after all, to believe that it was both foolish and unjust that landowners should earn vast sums at the public expense without doing anything in return. As even the authors of a minority report taking issue with Kenny's conclusions stressed, 'We do not think that a situation should continue where dealings in building land can result in large unearned profits for individuals and where local authorities have to compete with private interests in order to acquire land required for the expansion of towns and cities and to pay inflated prices for it . . .'

Kenny's recommendation was relatively straightforward: local authorities should be able to purchase compulsorily land in designated areas. The owners would be paid the current (agricultural) market value, plus a premium of 25 per cent. Kenny, a distinguished jurist, gave a detailed analysis of why and how his proposal could be fully compatible with Irish law and in particular with the rights of private property guaranteed by the Irish constitution.

There is a lovely Italian phrase: *dolce far niente*, the sweetness of doing nothing. The Italians presumably adapted it from Irish politics. In the case of the Kenny report, with its admirably concrete and sensible solution, the political establishment managed a far, far more *niente* response than the most sun-stunned sybarite, luxuriating in a Sardinian hammock, could ever muster. Faced with Kenny's unpalatable conclusions, those in power made a coma look like manic activity.

The way of dealing with the Kenny report was not to attack it or to defend the rights of landowners to make unearned fortunes and of property speculators to build up huge private land banks. It was simply to ignore it and, whenever anyone raised the subject, to say that it was under consideration. All parties in government at any given time agreed in principle with Kenny. All managed to believe that this conviction was like agreeing with Pythagoras' theorem – it was clearly right but you didn't have to do anything about it.

Here is a typical Dáil exchange on the subject, in May 1980, plucked from a profusion of available examples:

Mr F. O'Brien asked the Minister for the Environment
his proposals for the implementation of the Kenny Report
on land.

MR [GER] CONNOLLY [Minister for the Environment]:
Possible methods of dealing with outstanding problems
on building land costs are under consideration in my
Department in conjunction with other interested Departments. I will not be in a position to formulate my proposals until consideration of the complex problem involved
is finalised.

MR F. O'BRIEN: We have had this reply before. Could the
Minister give some indication of when we may have some
measures on land before the House for discussion?

MR CONNOLLY: When I came to the Department the first
thing I had a look at was the matter raised by the Deputy.
It is a complex issue and I am awaiting a number of views
on it. I do not want any undue delay.

MR F. O'BRIEN: Is it lack of will on the part of the
government or constitutional impediment that is causing
these inordinately long delays? This has been dragging
on since 1973.

MR CONNOLLY: I admit it has but I am unable to go
further than saying I am having the whole position examined. I assure the Deputy I am as concerned as anybody
else about the cost of building land and everything connected with it as regards housing.

MR F. O'BRIEN: Is the problem a constitutional one or is
it a lack of will on the part of the government?

MR CONNOLLY: It is a complex issue.

MR F. O'BRIEN: Is it a constitutional issue?

MR CONNOLLY: That is a matter for legal interpretation . . .

During the boom years, when it was obvious that vast fortunes were being made by landowners because of public zoning decisions and on the backs of hard-pressed house-buyers, everyone in the political system agreed that it was long past time that the Kenny report was implemented.

In 2000, Bertie Ahern, pretending to respond to public concern over rapidly rising house prices, asked the All-Party Oireachtas Committee on the Constitution, chaired by the future Minister for Finance Brian Lenihan, to go back over the ground covered by Kenny and his committee. Unsurprisingly, they came to exactly the same conclusions as had been reached in 1973: that Kenny was right to suggest the compulsory purchase of development land at a price modestly above the agricultural value, and that there was no constitutional problem about doing this. The committee had heard pleas to implement Kenny's proposals from powerful official bodies like the National Roads Authority and the Railway Procurement Agency (both fed up with paying extortionate prices for land needed for transport infrastructure) and Forfas, the official advisory body for enterprise and science.

The chances that something so obviously and urgently in the public interest would actually be implemented, however, were as remote as the dark side of Pluto. Kenny threatened just one small group of people – the speculators and developers who controlled the land banks. Unfortunately, Fianna Fáil would sooner have personally insulted the Pope, Nelson Mandela and Mother Teresa before it would offend that very group. Which was not o say, of course, that it was not committed to implementing the Kenny report. As late as 2006, Bertie Ahern was still declaring his intention to bring in legislation to control the price of development land. It was cruel happenstance and downright misfortune that he never got round to it.

Nor did he even get round to the more modest measures suggested by his own consultants to rein in the flagrant self-enrichment of this tiny minority of landowners and property speculators. Peter Bacon and Associates, commissioned by the government to study the inflation of house prices in the late 1990s, recommended an 'anti-speculation property tax' to stop people buying houses purely for investment purposes. The proposal was modest enough – an annual tax of 2 to 3 per cent of the value of the property. It was resolutely ignored.

Even the simplest of measures to bring some transparency to the operation of the market in land and property were not implemented. Almost every civilised country has a registry of land and property transactions, so that the public can see who is buying what and how much they're paying. In Ireland, this information was deliberately kept secret. The Kenny report pointed out that 'Any member of the public should be able to find out what prices have been paid for land and the nature of the dealings in it. Under the law as it is now, this is not possible.' It suggested simple changes to the law to make this 'essential' information available. The Oireachtas All-Party Committee repeated this call: 'In order to encourage transparency in property markets and research, transaction details should be gathered and published by the state. All lands and titles should be registered by a specified date. Auctioneers and estate agents, who generate, supply and promote market information, should be regulated by either an independent body or the state.'

None of this was done. The government allowed dealings in land and property to remain veiled in secrecy, so that land prices could be more easily manipulated and house prices inflated by estate-agent puffery.

This determination to do nothing was not the result of mere laziness. It was ideologically driven. It stemmed from two related shifts in attitude. One was a move away from the old idea that public policy should be guided by the basic aim of allowing as many people as possible access to affordable housing. So long as this basic belief held sway, it followed that relatively cheap housing was a good thing and that sharp rises in house prices were bad. Especially after Bertie Ahern, Charlie McCreevy and Mary Harney came to power in 1997, the government stopped believing this.

Part of the problem was, of course, that Fianna Fáil was very close to the people who gained most from high property prices – the builders and developers. Another part, however, was the self-generating nature of a demand for expensive houses. Ireland gradually became a nation of speculators, betting on endless rises in house prices. People who already had houses at the start of the boom had an interest in seeing their values rise. People who bought houses at inflated prices acquired the same interest. The more people who were suckered into borrowing beyond their means to acquire houses for up to twice their real worth, the larger the critical mass of voters for whom the idea of the government acting to make housing cheaper was anathema. Quite simply, cheap housing was good if you didn't have a house and bad if you did. And in a nation of house owners, the second category was bigger and grew faster than the first. Between 1995 and 2008, around 1.1 million mortgages for house purchases were approved – a very large chunk of the electorate who had bought property in the boom years.

Working alongside this growth in the property-owning or at least property-mortgaging class was another ideological shift – towards the market as the solution to all problems.

One of the things that had traditionally helped to control house prices in Ireland was the fact that a large proportion of dwellings were built by local authorities. Housing was understood to be a social need first and a commodity second. Thus, in the mid-1940s, 70 per cent of all new housing in the state was built by local councils and city corporations. With the spread of property mania, however, housing became first and foremost a commodity or an investment. Drunk on the orthodoxy that the market was best placed to deliver this commodity, the Fianna Fáil/Progressive Democrat governments began to cut off the supply of public housing. From 27 per cent in 1985, the share of local authority housing in the overall production of new homes sank to just 6 per cent. Lip service continued to be paid to social housing, in the form of targets for 35,000 local authority houses in the first National Development Plan, but only 21,000 were actually built.

The grotesque irony was that, during a period when the main activity of the country seemed to be the building of houses, there were more and more people who didn't have, and could not afford to buy or rent, a decent home. The number of people officially recognised as being in unfit or overcrowded accommodation, homeless or unable to afford a house, increased by 105 per cent between 1996 and 2008. In the midst of a vast housing boom, there were over 100,000 households or about 236,000 people struggling to keep an adequate roof over their heads.

By an even grimmer irony, this figure was quite similar to the number of surplus houses produced by a hysterical private housing market in overdrive. Michael Punch showed that between 1996 and 2006, there were 347,000 new households formed in Ireland. Over the same period, 597,000 new houses were built. This suggests that 250,000 houses were not built to meet housing needs but were either second homes or investment vehicles. Second or investment homes went up in some areas like mushrooms: 30 per cent of the homes in Leitrim were vacant on the night of the 2006 census. But even in Dublin one house in every eight was vacant.

The main government response to this absurdity was to add another delicious twist of farce. It instituted an 'affordable homes' scheme, under which builders and local authorities would work together to provide houses for those who could not get large mortgages from banks. This involved a double irony. In the first place, the designation of a small numbers of houses (between 2 and 4 per cent of the total) as affordable logically implied that all the other houses were unaffordable. No one paid much attention to this obvious truth. In the second place, and in a gesture beyond satire, tens of thousands of people who applied for affordable homes were turned down on the basis that they were too poor to afford them.

The property boom also produced another paradoxical novelty in Irish life – people who'd never had so much money and who were never in so much debt. As the boom went on and the property frenzy outstripped the seventeenth-century Tulip Mania, the mismatch between the earnings of ordinary workers and the cost of housing could be dealt with only by borrowing money for very long periods. People were buying what they thought of as their 'first home', often in a place they didn't want to live in for very long, but locking themselves into thirty-year mortgages to pay for it. Between 2004 and 2007, at the height of the madness, the proportion of first-time buyers taking out a mortgage of over thirty years rose from 29 per cent to 75 per cent. Mortgages of 100 per cent, and even 110 per cent of the cost price, became commonplace. Even in 2008, when the credit crunch had come and the collapse of the Irish property market was looming, over a quarter of first-time buyers were given 100 per cent mortgages by their banks or building societies.

Especially in the last four years of the boom, Ireland became the owe-zone of Europe. The housing boom fuelled a vertiginous growth in private sector credit. This was already very high by the end of the 1990s – around 110 per cent of GNP in 1999, which was higher than the proportion in Scandinavian countries when their banking systems had collapsed earlier in the decade. Especially after 2001, when the European Central Bank made sharp cuts in interest rates, things got far worse. In 2004, private credit stood at €190 billion – 145 per cent of GNP. In 2006, it was €305 billion – more than double the size of GNP. By 2008, it had hit the €400 billion mark – two and a half times GNP. Property-related lending amounted to about two-thirds of this vast swamp of credit.

The annual rate of growth of private sector credit in Ireland in 2006 (€65 billion in one year alone) is probably the highest in any country anywhere, ever. A big part of this was created by people taking out mortgages. The level of personal mortgage debt in Ireland increased by €2 billion *a month* during 2006, a year in which the average price of a new house in Dublin rose by €55,000 in 12 months. Both personal debt and mortgage debt doubled in the five years between 2004 and 2008.

Much of this debt was essentially a transfer of wealth from the putative future incomes of ordinary workers to the bank accounts of those who had gained control of the property development industry. But it was also creating an obvious instability in the Irish economy as a whole. As early as 22 December 1999, Standard and Poor's *Credit Week* mentioned Ireland as one of seven countries with a financial system vulnerable to a credit bust.

In an article in the February 2000 edition of *Finance* magazine, the former Central Bank regulator William Slattery pointed to the unsustainable nature of the growth in private sector credit. Sooner or later, he argued, borrowing would have to come back to a rational level, and when it did so, this would 'result in the removal of the source of a large volume of expenditure in the economy. When this happens I believe it is likely that the supply of property will substantially exceed demand . . . In that event, a substantial decline in property prices is inevitable.' How much would prices fall? Given the inflated prices being charged for houses and land, Slattery's educated guess was that 'A return to more normal levels for each of these elements would mean a substantial drop in house prices, perhaps as much as 30 to 50 per cent.' Unless the government made it a priority to ensure that house prices did not continue to rise, Slattery warned, it would simply 'exacerbate what I believe is likely to be ultimately a quite traumatic situation for many current house buyers'. This is pretty much what happened: the government did not try to stop house prices rising, prices ultimately dropped by 30 to 50 per cent and it was indeed pretty traumatic for people who had bought homes during the boom years.

To be fair, it is something of a misrepresentation to say that the government did not try to control the property boom. Bertie Ahern remarked in 2006 that 'the boom is getting more boomier', and making booms boomier was what Fianna Fáil did. Faced with a rapidly inflating balloon it took the advice that Lauren Bacall gave to Humphrey Bogart in *To Have and Have Not*: 'Just pucker up your lips and blow.'

The Bacallian (or should that be Bacchanalian?) school of economics, as perfected by Ahern, McCreevy and Harney, dictated that the way to make sure that a property crash did not destroy the economy was to force-feed property developers and investors with tax incentives. The government created a bewildering array of property-based tax breaks to encourage more building, higher land prices, and a diversion of potentially productive investment into yet more bricks and mortar. There were incentives for the developers of hotels and holiday camps, of private hospitals and nursing homes, of holiday cottage schemes, of third-level educational buildings and student accommodation blocks, of childcare and park-and-ride facilities, of multi-storey car parks and refurbished flats. Most of this was stark stupidity: the number of hotel rooms, for example, increased by 150 per cent in the Celtic Tiger years, while the number of tourists increased by 70 per cent. Developers were building hotels, not to meet a market demand, but simply to get the tax subsidies from the government. Fianna Fáil ended up spending €330 million of public money to subsidise the building of hotels. The only effect was to make the hotel trade unviable. With so many of them sprouting up all over the place, there were simply not enough paying guests to go round. By the summer of 2009, Irish hotels, with an occupancy rate of 53 per cent, were officially half-empty – a towering achievement for Bacallian economics.

One of the most popular tax incentives was the so-called Section 23 relief, under which most of the cost of building rental accommodation (generally apartment blocks) in designated areas could be set against tax. The original intention was that the relief would encourage development in specific, neglected urban areas. It was rapidly seized on as a broad tax-avoidance measure. Ruairi Quinn, then the outgoing Finance minister in the Rainbow Coalition government defeated by Bertie Ahern in 1997, told a story of that year's election. He was canvassing in Carrick-on-Shannon in County Leitrim for the local Labour Party candidate. Leitrim is one of the least urbanised areas in Western Europe. Quinn was approached by members of the Carrick-on-Shannon Chamber of Commerce. 'They said, "We want section 23" and I asked what part of Carrick-on-Shannon they wanted it for, to which they replied, "Oh no, we don't want to make a selection." I asked what other places they wanted and was told: "We don't want to be competitive between one town or one village and another." I asked them what exactly they would like and they said, "We want you to give section 23 to the whole of County Leitrim."'

This helps to explain why Leitrim ended up with almost one in three of its houses empty and with hundreds of houses built in villages like Dromod or Leitrim village that recorded only a very small increase in their actual population. It is a strange housing boom that leaves such places literally emptier than they were before.

The state ended up subsidising – to the tune of around €2 billion in all – the building of houses whose purpose was to provide shelter, not for real people, but for the taxes of their builders. The tax costs to the state of the various 'renewal' schemes amounted to a staggering 43 per cent of the cost of the actual developments. Instead of providing real houses for people who desperately needed them, €2 billion of public money was squandered on putting up empty shells in places where no one wanted to live.

These were, almost without exception, state subsidies for the rich. Indecon, from whom the government eventually commissioned an analysis of the property-based tax incentives, concluded that 'nearly all of the property tax incentives reviewed have been used primarily by high income earners'. None was introduced as a result of a cost/benefit analysis. None was time-limited, so that incentives that might perhaps make some sense at a particular moment continued to operate long after they were remotely justifiable.

What the incentives did achieve, however, was to help turn Ireland from a society in which construction serviced the economy into one in which the economy existed to service construction. In May 2009, in a half-hearted excuse for an apology, the Taoiseach Brian Cowen, who had been a pitifully compliant minister for finance during the worst of the bubble years, regretted the 'reliance on the construction sector, which had grown to 12% of GDP'. This in itself was an interesting example of Freudian repression. The construction sector wasn't 12 per cent of GDP. It was, at the height of the boom in 2006, almost 24 per cent of GDP. This was twice the average ratio for Western Europe. It directly accounted in 2006 for 19 per cent of the entire workforce. In other words, a quarter of all the economic activity in the state was the manipulation of bricks and mortar, concrete and tarmac. One person in five was employed in building the houses, roads, office blocks and infrastructure for the other four to live in, work in and travel through.

The height of absurdity was reached in the last years of the boom when Ireland was importing construction workers from Central and Eastern Europe to build the houses in which they themselves would live. In 2006, 13 per cent of the workforce in Irish construction was made up of migrant workers. Many builders were relying on these workers to rent the houses the last wave of migrant workers had built , while they themselves built the houses for the expected next wave of central European builders to rent.

Faced with this looming disaster, and its implications for the stability of the banking sector, the Central Bank stood on the sidelines wringing its hands. Its own figures, published in its annual stability reports, were terrifying: bank lending for construction and real estate grew from €5.5 billion in 1999 to €96.2 billion in 2007 – an increase of 1,730 per cent. On average, this lending was growing by 18 per cent *a month*. Even if the Irish regulators didn't concern themselves with awkward things like ethics and legality, they were supposed to be in the business of risk management and banking stability. That the pace and scale of this rise in lending to one sector of the economy met with no real regulatory response suggests a mass migration to the Republic of Catatonia.

In May 2009, Brian Cowen claimed that he and the government had been well aware all along that construction and property had become cuckoos in the economic nest and had been planning to tackle the problem. 'The reliance on the construction sector was something we were in fact going to move down, over time, to get a soft landing'. Apart from the obvious fact that these good intentions were never acted on, one reason to doubt whether Fianna Fáil had the will to act is that the construction and property boom had become essential to the party's very being.

Fianna Fáil, in the boom years, had to juggle two ideological imperatives. On the one hand, it had bought into the so-called free market agenda of low taxes for individuals and corporations as the mainstay of economic prosperity. On the other, it remained a populist party with the need to satisfy a large and diverse electoral base that included much of the urban working class and welfare recipients and also many rural and provincial communities who expected their politicians to deliver public goods to the local area. How could it choose between low taxes and the concomitant of poor social services on the one side and the need to keep low-income and regional voters reasonably happy on the other? In order to avoid that choice, it needed to pull off the trick of simultaneously cutting taxes and increasing spending. The magical substance that allowed it to achieve this apparently impossible feat was concrete. The construction boom filled the gap between real, sustainable revenue and spendthrift, careless spending. It meant that Fianna Fáil did not have to do the one thing against which every fibre in its republican being revolted: make a choice.

Money flowed into the state coffers from the construction boom through stamp duty, VAT on construction materials, capital-related taxes and income taxes on building workers, including those who came into the country from Central Europe. VAT on house building alone accounted for 8 per cent of Irish tax revenue in 2006. Overall, property-related taxes, which had contributed 4 per cent of government revenue in 1996, made up at least 17 per cent in 2006.

In real terms, taking out these unsustainable factors, the Irish public finances were in the red: the IMF calculated this 'structural deficit' at 9 per cent of GDP in 2007 and 12.5 per cent in 2008. But the construction-related revenues turned this deficit into a budget surplus, creating both the illusion that there was plenty of money to spend and a lack of concern with how well it was spent.

The government turned itself into a junkie, injecting itself every day with the narcotic of easy money from the property bubble. Like every addict, its main interest was in making sure the supply of the drug didn't dry up. In these circumstances, two things were inevitable. One was that the bubble of debt and inflated property values would burst with, as Slattery had predicted, 'traumatic' consequences for those who had bought houses at the top of the market. The other was that this first inevitability would be denied, ignored and, if possible, obliterated from the public mind.

Thus, in late 2006, when Morgan Kelly, professor of economics at University College Dublin, wrote an extensive piece in the *Irish Times*, and followed it up with an academic paper with the phlegmatically chilling title 'On The Likely Extent of Falls in Irish House Prices', he might as well have broken wind in an airtight room. Kelly made the point that he had studied forty booms and busts in property markets in OECD countries since 1970. The overall pattern is remarkably stable: property loses 70 per cent of the value it gained during the bubble years. There is a simple law: the more house prices rise relative to average incomes, the harder they will fall. On this basis, Irish house prices were due to fall by between 40 and 60 per cent.

This was not a wild jeremiad. This kind of fall had happened in Holland in the 1980s, in Switzerland and Norway in the late 1980s, and in Finland in the early 1990s. These slumps, and the others that Kelly detailed, were typically quite long in duration: five to seven years was the norm, but the markets in Switzerland, Japan and Holland had taken at least a decade to recover.

Kelly cut through the favoured phrase of government, cheerleader economists, banks and property companies – 'soft landing' – like a scalpel through silk:

. . . a soft landing is not so much unlikely as contradict-ory. Suppose that house prices really were expected to level off, then the owners of the tens of thousands of empty houses and apartments can expect no further capi-tal gains and should cash in their investments. Why pay a mortgage on an empty apartment that has stopped rising in value? As speculators rush for the exit, prices will crash.

Second, if prices stop rising, it makes no sense to buy a house. Compared with mortgages, rents are ridiculously low. For €2,000 a month you can pay a mortgage on something in a muddy field on the wrong side of Cel-bridge [in the commuter belt south of Dublin], without nearby shops or schools and a two-hour commute to Dublin. For the same amount you can rent a €1 million house in southeast Dublin, close to the Dart [rapid rail] line and surrounded by good schools. Once people put off buying in favour of renting, prices will not stabilise, they will crash.

The effects on an economy dangerously dependent on con-struction would, he warned, be catastrophic: 'We could see a collapse of government revenue and unemployment back above 15 per cent.'

Bertie Ahern's response to Kelly's (entirely accurate) pre-dictions was to urge him and his ilk to kill themselves. 'Sit-ting on the sidelines, cribbing and moaning is a lost opportunity. I don't know how people who engage in that don't commit suicide.' Ahern got strong support from his main media cheerleader, the bestselling Sunday newspaper the *Sunday Independent*, whose deputy editor Liam Collins wrote that 'Bertie Ahern got it absolutely right' and attacked the Economic and Social Research Institute for having the bad taste even to publish Kelly's paper: 'The state-funded Economic & Social Research Institute set the stalled ball rolling again last week when it regurgitated a hysterical rant from an academic who had the audacity to accuse those in the property business of "wishful thinking" because they remained optimistic about the future of house prices. Professor Morgan Kelly, from the bloated campus of University College Dublin, first jumped on the property bandwagon on December 21, 2006, with his paper, *Irish House Prices: Gliding into the Abyss?* When not too many people paid much attention to his thesis, the state "think tank" reissued his gloom-laden forecast under the new guise of academic research. It came with complicated formulae, big words and long, hard-to-read paragraphs – but the same dismal conclusions.' Collins accused Kelly of 'tabloid scholarship'.

What was remarkable, however, was how few mainstream economists came to Kelly's defence. Every historically literate economist knew for sure that the Irish property boom was going to crash. As early as August 2000, the International Monetary Fund put the Irish bubble in the context of all known modern property booms and concluded that 'there has not been a single experience of price inflation on the scale of Ireland's which did not end in prices falling'. Given that prices actually doubled in the six years after that warning, the scale of the crash was even more predictable. Yet the overwhelming majority of Irish economists either contented themselves with timid and carefully couched murmurs of unease or, in the case of most of those who worked for stockbrokers, banks and building societies and who dominated media discussions of the issue, joined in the reassurances about soft landings.

In effect, the cheerleaders for the Celtic Tiger had constructed an impregnable but entirely fictional reality. It was an unquestionable certainty as secure as the Tsar's conviction that there could be no revolution in Russia or Donald Rumsfeld's conviction that there were weapons of mass destruction in Iraq. In a country that was losing its religion, the indestructibility of the property market was the remaining one true faith. Were it not for the unfortunate restrictions of modern civility, heretics like Kelly would have been burned at the stake in O'Connell Street. Unreality was now the place where Ireland lived.

6

Kings of the Wild Frontier

'Don't try to protect everyone from every possible accident'
– Charlie McCreevy

If, at the height of the Irish boom, you stopped virtually any-one in the street in Dublin and asked them the following questions, you could be pretty sure of the answers they would give:

(a) Where does most of the foreign investment in Ireland come from?

(b) What sectors of the economy does it go into?

(c) What is Ireland's largest bank?

The answers were common knowledge. Most of the invest-ment came from the United States of America. Most of it went into either information technology (Intel, Microsoft, IBM) or pharmaceuticals (Pfizer, Eli Lilly, Merck). And Ire-land's largest bank was Allied Irish.

In fact, these obvious answers were all wrong. From 2002 onwards, the largest source of foreign direct investment into Ireland was the Netherlands (€10.7 billion that year, com-pared to €7.9 billion from the USA). In 2003, €8.6 billion came from the Netherlands, while flows from the US were actually negative, with more going out in repatriated profits than came in through investment. Even in 2007, when North American investment doubled to €31 billion, it was still less than the €33 billion that came from the Netherlands.

Where was this vast Dutch investment coming from? Was

Shell oil buying up the entire country? Were the Dutch rat-race refuseniks who set up smallholdings in rural Ireland in the 1970s planning an unimaginable expansion of their organic cheese-making operations? In fact the money was mostly connected to high-level financial juggling by American-owned transnational corporations, with their Dutch-based treasury-management subsidiaries routing capital flows through Dublin.

The answer to the second question was equally surprising. The largest single component of the stock of foreign-owned assets in Ireland was not in either information technology or pharmaceuticals, it was in the International Financial Services Centre (IFSC) in Dublin, which is essentially a tax haven for global finance. The prominence of world-leading transnational firms like Intel or Pfizer may have defined the Irish economic landscape. Their presence was solid and reassuring – whatever anyone thought of them, however much we knew about their repatriation of vast profits every year, they were global industrial titans, producing real products for real export markets. But they were dwarfed by the sheer scale of money that was pumped through the IFSC. In 2005, for example, the IFSC accounted for approximately 75 per cent of all foreign investment in Ireland. Yet it was not particularly surprising that most Irish people would not have known this, for it was not easy to understand exactly what many of the companies in the IFSC were up to.

And, to answer the third question, the largest Irish bank was not AIB, but the giant German operation Depfa (short for Deutsche Pfandbriefanstalt), a specialist lender to governments and municipalities that transferred its global headquarters to the IFSC in Dublin in 2002. Its global centre at Harbourmaster Place on the River Liffey had just 319 employees, but claimed assets in 2003 of $218 billion. Depfa had been as German as sauerkraut – it was founded by the Prussian government in 1922 and it was still listed on the Frankfurt stock exchange. But it was now as Irish as bacon and cabbage.

The IFSC was established in 1987 by Charles Haughey, at the suggestion of one his financial backers, Dermot Desmond, specifically to persuade international finance companies to set up offices in a new, American-designed development at Custom House Docks on the Liffey, just a few minutes east of Dublin's city centre. The incentive was simple: a 10 per cent rate of corporation tax. (The IFSC moved in 2005 to a 12.5 per cent tax rate and companies were allowed to locate themselves outside the Custom House Docks centre.)

The IFSC worked. It attracted half of the world's top fifty banks and top twenty insurance companies, alongside another 1,200 operations of various sizes. By 2003, Ireland was the main global location for money market mutual funds (a total of $125 billion in these funds was domiciled in Dublin), overtaking its old spiritual hinterland of the Cayman Islands. In the same year, Dublin's investment funds industry (valued at $480 billion) surpassed London's. Hedge fund managers liked the place: by 2004, over $200 billion in hedge fund assets were being serviced in Dublin.

The IFSC eventually employed 25,000 people, many of them on high salaries. In spite of the low tax rate, it contributed, at its height in 2006, €1.2 billion in taxes to the government. But there was a price to pay for these blessings. The attraction of the IFSC for the global finance industry was not just low taxation. It was also lax, and in some cases virtually non-existent, regulation. The Irish state acquired an incentive to keep banking supervision to a minimum.

Any urge to beef up regulation after the DIRT and Ansbacher scandals was outweighed by the belief that the Irish tradition of looking the other way while banks passed funny money around was actually an economic asset. Ethitical banking went global. While the embodiment of Irish banking culture had been the bogus non-resident, now it became the bogus resident. The unreality of Irish people pretending to be elsewhere was replaced by the unreality of foreign people pretending to be in Ireland.

In February 2009, the *Guardian* newspaper sent reporters to Dublin to check out the 'head offices' of British companies that were now 'domiciled' in Ireland: 'One such "headquarters" turned out to be merely the premises of the company's accountants. Other multi-nationals had just a handful of staff at work, no nameplates outside, or occupied the premises only sporadically . . . Tarsus, a business media group, says its new Irish headquarters is in a redeveloped Dublin dock by the river Liffey. But when we went there, it appeared to be merely the premises of their tax advisers, PWC [Price Waterhouse Coopers]. Henderson Global Investors has only three staff at its Dublin suite of off-the-shelf rental offices, compared with 550 who continue to work at its main London office. A receptionist in Ireland said: 'They are not here a lot of the time.' Charter Engineers has no nameplate on its temporary offices, and the company secretary – one of only five staff – flies in on Monday and home again on Friday.'

Under Irish tax law, a corporation can pay its entire tax bill in Ireland if 'its central management and control are located in the state'. The ghostly presences traced by the *Guardian* are the ciphers of 'central management and control' that allow companies to pay tax at generous Irish rates

rather than more stringent British ones. The *Guardian* revelations prompted the Treasury spokesman of the Liberal
Democrats to call Dublin 'Lichtenstein on the Liffey'.

If the Irish had a right to be insulted by this description, it
was only because we tended to prefer warmer, Caribbean
climes. The Cayman Islands, as we have seen, was a virtual
fifth province in the 1980s. And in fact, the official equivalent that the IFSC was seeking was also West Indian: in 2003,
referring to the IFSC, the state's Industrial Development
Agency (IDA) actually boasted that 'There has been rapid
growth in the Irish insurance and reinsurance industries in
recent years, with Dublin fast becoming the Bermuda of
Europe.'

While much relatively straightforward banking business
was done at the IFSC, two aspects of what went on there
were fraught with long-term danger for Ireland. The first was
the construction of this outlandish volume of fictions, the
creation of a parallel universe of apparently vast financial
operations with huge paper assets but almost no substance.
Dublin became the Potemkin village of global finance.

The main force behind the creation of this shadow economy was the attraction to Dublin of the treasury management
arms of transnational corporations (TNCs). The purpose of
these companies is to rationalise the flows of capital between
different parts of a global group and, of course, to ensure
that the overall tax bill is as meagre as the magic of financial
wizardry can make it. The IFSC, with its low corporation tax
rates, tax exemptions on dividends and interest payments,
and access to Ireland's large range of bilateral tax treaties,
was attractive in this light. The 12.5 per cent tax rate was a
little over a third of that prevailing in the US and most of
Western Europe. By 2002, Ireland had become the single

largest location of declared pre-tax profits for US firms (followed, aptly, by Bermuda).

The other attraction, though, was the lack of regulation, or what the IDA called 'a flexible and business focused tax and regulatory system'. In the case of treasury management operations, the business-focused regulatory system had two aspects. Firstly, these treasury arms of TNCs were allowed to set themselves up as banks. And secondly, the Central Bank and its supervisory arm (known firstly as the Irish Financial Services Authority and then as the Financial Regulator) agreed not to regulate them.

As the IDA put it for the benefit of potential clients: 'In 1998, the Regulator revised its Bank licensing regulations and it may now accept, under certain circumstances, applications from corporate entities to be licensed as Banks. In the case of most group treasury and asset financing operations the Regulator has disapplied its powers of supervision.' The word 'disapplied' was a wonderful Irish coinage. Global corporations, in other words, could establish unsupervised banks in Dublin. At the height of the boom, there were over 400 of these firms at the IFSC – there are now around 350.

These entities were usually subsidiaries of subsidiaries, owned by companies that the corporations had already established in other countries, many of them tax havens or low-tax jurisdictions. (In thirty-two of the forty-six cases that Trinity College Dublin economist Jim Stewart studied, the parent company of the Irish operation was located in a tax haven.) Thus, 3Com IFSC, the Irish affiliate of 3Com, is registered in the Cayman Islands; Kinsale Financial Services, the IFSC offshoot of Eli Lilly, is registered in Switzerland; Pfizer International Bank Europe is registered in the Isle of Man, and Brangate, the IFSC arm of Tyco, is registered in

Luxembourg. Some of these companies were like Babushka dolls: Xerox Leasing is the Irish subsidiary of a Jersey subsidiary of a Greek subsidiary of the US photocopy machine manufacturer.

These convoluted structures were not accidental. One of the measures proposed by the Obama presidency in the US in 2009, for example, was to permit transnational corporations to have only one layer of subsidiary ownership for tax purposes. The accompanying Congressional memorandum on tax havens specifically cited Ireland: 'Thus, a U.S. parent with a subsidiary in Ireland could treat that subsidiary as a branch (disregard it as a separate entity). The Irish subsidiary, however, could not treat its German subsidiary as a disregarded entity.' The amount of money at stake is obvious from the amount of tax the US authorities expected to raise in a single year from this one measure: $86.5 billion.

For the most part, these Irish operations were front companies, with huge assets and almost no employees. Jim Stewart did a detailed study of treasury management firms in Ireland between 1998 and 2005. He was able to work out figures for forty-eight of them. The results were startling. Most had no fixed (as opposed to financial) assets and most paid no fees to directors, implying that those directors actually worked elsewhere. These were virtual entities, existing in a financial version of Second Life.

In the year 2000, for example, the firms in Stewart's study had combined assets of $48 billion. They employed a grand total of 128 people: fewer than four employees each. In 2005, the firms had median gross assets of $643 million each. They had a grand total of seventy-five employees – on average, fewer than two each. (Twenty-eight of the forty-six had no employees at all.) With assets of $320 million dollars per job, those employees were so productive they made Stakhanov look like a slacker. Statistically, in fact, as Stewart reported, 'the median number employed was zero for each of the years 1999–2005 and just one employee for the year 1998'.

A not untypical example was Eli Lilly's IFSC wing, Kinsale Financial Services. In 2004, it had profits of $96 million, after paying a dividend of $8.6 million to its US parent and $13.6 million taxes to the Irish state. It employed precisely two people. From the Irish government's perspective, these firms were generating tax revenue but providing practically no employment.

They were, however, very useful vehicles for the transnational corporations. Their Dublin-based financial arms were able to shift huge piles of untaxed money out to the shareholders of their parent companies. For example, in 1999 alone, Brangate Limited, an IFSC-based subsidiary of the notorious American corporation Tyco, paid out a dividend of $6.6 billion. A subsidiary of Johnson and Johnson located in Ireland repatriated a dividend of €6.7 billion in 2005. Aggregate dividend outflows and distributed profits from Ireland rose from $13.2 billion in 2003 to $25.7 billion in 2006. When, in 2004, the US allowed its firms a 'repatriation holiday' during which they could bring in dividends from abroad at a very low tax rate, Ireland was the fourth largest source of the money that flowed in, after Holland, Switzerland and Bermuda.

For the Irish state, this whole operation seemed straightforward enough. In return for housing these front companies and allowing their parents to avoid taxes in their home countries, Ireland got no jobs, but it did get the tax revenue. Essentially, the deal was that the front companies would pony up 12.5 per cent of profits in corporation tax and the state would neither look too closely at its activities nor listen to the complaints of the foreign governments whose exchequers were losing out.

The problem, however, was that if there are vast amounts of money flowing around and no one is watching, the results are predictable. Fiction shades into fraud.

Eurofood IFSC Limited was a classic denizen of the Bahamian outpost beyond O'Connell Bridge. Established at the IFSC in 1997, it had no fixed assets, and no employees, but reported pre-tax earnings of $48 million between 1997 and 2002. It had net financial assets of almost $200 million, but its registered office was simply that of a leading firm of solicitors, McCann FitzGerald. One director was a partner in that legal firm. Another was an employee of Bank of America, which acted as Eurofood's agent and effectively did all of its work. The other two directors were senior executives of Eurofood's parent company, the Italian food conglomerate Parmalat, and lived in Italy.

Eurofood, in other words, was a typical IFSC front company. As the Irish Supreme Court put it: 'The Company's policy was decided at Parmalat headquarters in Italy, by Parmalat executives, and the Company exercised no independent decision-making function.' Yet, as the Irish and European courts later ruled, Eurofood was an Irish company, subject to Irish law and, in theory at least, regulated by the Department of Finance, the Central Bank and the Financial Regulator.

According to the same Supreme Court ruling, the Italian directors did not always bother to attend the meetings of Eurofood's board but 'sometimes communicated by telephone'. One of the Italian directors was recorded as being present on six occasions but on the phone for four meetings. The other was physically present on five occasions and participating by phone on four others. Some of the Irish directors were likewise recorded at times as participating 'by phone'.

Yet this board took some very important decisions. Specifically, on one day in September 1998, it approved two huge transactions: the issuing of $80 million to Venezuelan companies in the Parmalat group and of $100 million to 'fund a loan by the Company to Brazilian companies in the Parmalat group'. These transactions were supposedly governed by Irish regulatory authorities and by Irish tax law.

Parmalat collapsed in late 2003 and went into administration. What emerged, according to the US Securities and Exchange Commission, was 'one of the largest and most brazen corporate financial frauds in history'. A $4.9 billion Parmalat account with Bank of America, which the company claimed to have stowed in the Cayman Islands, did not exist. Parmalat turned out to have debts of $14 billion, more than double what it declared on its balance sheet.

To hide the debt, Parmalat simply transferred the liabilities to subsidiaries based in offshore havens. According to Enrico Bondi, the Italian bankruptcy commissioner, 'In an attempt to hide its state of insolvency, Parmalat entangled itself in grandiose financial operations that were ever more costly.' Eurofood, which managed Parmalat's financial operations, was a crucial part of this operation. According to a spokesman for Parmalat's post-collapse administrators, 'Eurofood was deeply involved in the fraud at Parmalat . . . A large portion of the fraud involving Parmalat was at offshore vehicles where there was little or no transparency.'

Fausto Tonna, one of Eurofood's directors, was sentenced

to thirty months in jail in Italy in 2005, having pleaded guilty to playing a leading part in the company's spectacular scheme of faking of its accounts. The other director, Luciano Del Soldato, also pleaded guilty to fraud and got a twenty-two-month sentence. The chairman of McCann FitzGerald, the Irish law firm that had provided Eurofood with space for its brass plate and the statutory Irish resident for its board, described the episode as a case of 'being in the wrong place at the wrong time'.

By itself, the Parmalat case should have been a warning that the lax regime at the IFSC was wide open to abuse. There was, however, another area of concern, and it arose from one of the success stories of the IFSC, its ability to attract a large slice of the global reinsurance market. By 2003, 10 per cent of that worldwide market was underwritten in Dublin. This success was not based on the joys of the Irish weather. It was rooted in the happy absence of regulation.

Ireland, on the one hand, piggybacked on European Union laws and standards, which provided companies setting up in Dublin with a secure protective framework in which to operate. On the other hand, it specialised in allowing those companies to do as they pleased. A remarkably open analysis by one of the leading Dublin business law firms, William Fry, written in 2004 to mark the fifteenth anniversary of the establishment of the IFSC, was upfront about this contradiction:

A look at the insurance and reinsurance sectors reveals that there is a great paradox surrounding the legal and regulatory landscape. On the one hand, it was the existence of a comprehensive legal framework in the form of the three generations of [European Union legislation on insurance] that fostered the growth of these sectors. On the other hand, the reinsurance sector thrived because the relative absence of legislation meant that reinsurers could establish in the IFSC without having to concern themselves about solvency margins, asset admissibility rules and authorisation delays . . . the reinsurance sector thrived in the IFSC partly because of the absence of regulation, which allows reinsurance operations to establish quickly and without incurring high costs. The absence of any regulation regarding the solvency margins to be maintained by reinsurers or the admissibility of assets provided a fertile environment for the growth of both the captive sector and the establishment of innovative coverage providers . . . a pure reinsurer established in Ireland is free to provide reinsurance to insurers in any other Member States of the EU, notwithstanding that there is no system of prior authorisation or ongoing supervision of such reinsurers. The Insurance Act 2000 continued (albeit on a more formal basis) the 'approval but no supervision' regime. The [Act] also permits the Irish Financial Services Authority to direct a reinsurance operation to cease writing business in certain stated circumstances. We are not aware that this 'nuclear option' has ever in fact been exercised, however, these powers represent a necessary safeguard for the regulator, because once established there is virtually no ongoing supervision of reinsurance operations.

When the *New York Times* reported in 2005 that 'Dublin has become known in the insurance industry as something of the Wild West of European finance', it was not exaggerating. The IFSC was a lawless frontier town in which the spoils of the reinsurance trade were up for grabs and the sheriff walked only on the sunny side of the street, tipping his hat to the decent folks and avoiding the gaze of the desperados. And the baddest outlaw was John Houldsworth.

Houldsworth worked for Cologne Re, a German reinsurance firm, and helped to establish its Dublin arm in the early 1990s. Cologne Re was then acquired by an American firm, General Re, which in turn was bought by Warren Buffett's Berkshire Hathaway. Houldsworth became the main man at Cologne Re's Alternative Solutions Group in Dublin. Unfortunately what the group was generally offering was an alternative to ethical behaviour.

Houldsworth first came to notice with his contribution to the largest single bankruptcy in Australian history, the collapse in March 2001 of the HIH Insurance Group. HIH had purchased its apparently profitable rival FAI in 1999. It turned out that FAI's profits were fictional. The company had been kept afloat through a series of reinsurance contracts, the most important of which was with General Re. It had been engineered in Dublin by Houldsworth. He and his colleagues worked a bit of fiscal magic to make FAI seem much more solvent than it was. According to the Australian Royal Commission of Inquiry that examined the scandal: 'a wide array of practices were employed to achieve these ends, among them the use of side letters setting out arrangements that negated the transfer of risk, the backdating of documents, the inclusions of sections of cover not intended to be called upon and the use of "triggers" for additional cover that were unrealistic. The word audacious comes to mind.' A Royal Commission source explained to Justin O'Brien, professor of corporate governance at Queensland University of Technology, that those who constructed the deal were 'skilful interior designers' papering over, not just cracks, but 'gaping holes'.

As a result of the scandal, Houldsworth and another Dublin-based executive of General Re, Tore Ellingson, were barred from the Australian securities and insurance industries for life. Houldsworth was not prosecuted because he refused to travel to Australia for a legal hearing. The Australian authorities did, however, inform the Irish regulator of the outcome of their investigations. This was the equivalent of the Medical Council in one country warning another jurisdiction that it had struck off a doctor for malpractice. The obvious imperative was to stop Houldsworth working in Dublin. The Irish authorities chose to do nothing.

In late 2000 and early 2001, predictably enough, Houldsworth and his Alternative Solutions Group in Dublin were at the centre of another scam. This time, it involved General Re and the largest US insurer, American Insurance Group (AIG). AIG had a problem with the declining level of its loss reserves – the money it stored away in case of a catastrophe. Concerns about the problem led to a sharp fall in its share price after the release of quarterly results in October 2000.

AIG was General Re's biggest customer. When AIG's chief executive Hank Greenberg approached his opposite number at General Re, the outlines of a solution were agreed. General Re would take out $500 million worth of 'insurance' with AIG against future earnings decline. The 'insurance', however, was to be purely fictional. There would be no premiums and no transfer of risk. The point was simply to deceive AIG's investors by making its books look $500 million better.

They knew where to look for the engineering of this scam: to the 'audacious' Houldsworth in Dublin's Dodge City. In any well-regulated environment, the whole transaction would have raised immediate suspicions. With any scrutiny, the scheme would have revealed itself to be bogus simply because there was no premium being paid. As the then attorney general of New York, Eliot Spitzer, put it in his subsequent indictment: 'GenRe did not pay premiums. And in fact AIG did not reinsure genuine risk. To the contrary, AIG paid General Re US$5 million, and the only genuine service performed by either party was that General Re created false and misleading documentation to satisfy Greenberg's illicit goals.' Or as Houldsworth was recorded as saying in a phone call to General Re in the US: 'If there's enough pressure on their end, they'll find ways to cook the books, won't they?'

The US Securities and Exchange Commission was damningly clear in its interpretation of what had happened: 'This case is not about the violation of technical accounting rules. It involves the deliberate or extremely reckless efforts by senior corporate officers of a facilitator company (General Re) to aid and abet senior management of an issuer (AIG) in structuring transactions, having no economic substance, that were designed solely for the unlawful purpose of achieving a specific, and false, accounting effect on the issuer's financial statements.'

Cooking the books at AIG meant that its share price was inflated. Those who bought shares at these artificial prices subsequently lost a total of over $500 million as they plunged again when the scandal emerged.

When the scam was uncovered in the US, Houldsworth was prosecuted – in the US – and pleaded guilty to charges of securities manipulation and the creation of false documents. (He co-operated with the authorities, testified against his co-conspirators and got probation, while five other executives from General Re and AIG went to jail.)

Strikingly, Houldsworth, whose crimes were committed in Dublin, was not prosecuted by the Irish authorities.

The Irish regulators had nothing at all to say about the case. The judge who sentenced Houldsworth and the others in the US remarked that 'if fraud is contemplated . . . these people will know that they will be investigated and prosecuted for their involvement'. In Ireland 'these people' continued to know that the likelihood would be that they would not be caught and that, if they were, the worst that might befall them would be an embarrassed silence.

The realisation that the IFSC had been involved in a spectacular tri-continental triple crown of dodgy dealing – Europe's biggest ever fraud, the largest bankruptcy in Australian history, and a $500 million scam in the US – meant that the Irish authorities surely had to react. They did – by bringing in more tax loopholes and corporate benefits and increasing their commitment to 'light touch' regulation.

Particularly after Houldsworth pleaded guilty in 2005, there were ominous signs that the scandals were doing real harm to Ireland's international reputation. The normally supportive International Monetary Fund began to make noises about the laxity of regulation in the Dublin reinsurance market. Justin O'Brien highlighted the IFSC's place in the Houldsworth scams in an article in the Australian *Journal of Corporate Law* and in a number of prescient pieces in the *Irish Times*. O'Brien warned that the scandals 'severely compromise the reputation of Ireland as an emergent financial services centre'. He quoted 'off-the-record briefings provided to the author by senior regulators in Australia and the United States throughout August 2005'. One expressed 'shock and dismay that Ireland had abdicated its responsibilities for short-term advantage'. Another said, 'good luck to

Ireland if it thinks it is going to get away with it, but it won't'.

The essential reaction of the Irish regulators, however, was denial. After the Australian authorities banned Houldsworth and Ellingson in 2004, the Regulator did nothing about the fact that they were still employed at Cologne Re in Dublin. In March 2005, when the AIG scam had already come to light, it publicly endorsed this state of affairs, claiming that Cologne Re had taken 'corrective action' in relation to the pair. On the one hand, said the Regulator's official spokesman, the authority was not empowered to take action against anyone except company directors. On the other hand, it claimed that in any case 'We are satisfied with the corrective actions in relation to these individuals that have been taken to date by Cologne Re and we will continue to actively monitor the situation.' He was unwilling or unable to say what that 'corrective action' was.

A few months later, the Regulator's chief executive Liam O'Reilly gave an interview to the *Irish Times* in which he said: 'We will never get rid of original sin. We all fall down at times. We are not in the business to make sure everyone who falls is punished. It is our job to make sure there are appropriate systems, processes and procedures in place.' He went on to imply that the Regulator had known about Houldsworth's 'audacious' adventures in Australia for a long time and had in fact acted to stop his activities in Dublin: 'There was an implication in the media that we were caught by surprise,' O'Reilly said. 'We knew about the issue well before it hit the papers. We were talking to regulators in Australia and the entity here. We had ensured these individuals were not in positions of power here. We are happy we dealt with it appropriately.' This was simply untrue: Houldsworth had been in a sufficient position of power to co-engineer a $500 million fraud.

If there was denial from the regulators, there was positive defiance from the politicians. Ireland 'declined to participate' in an International Monetary Fund programme to monitor offshore financial centres and their 'compliance with supervisory and integrity standards' – a quiet signal that business would go on as usual.

The 2004 Finance Act contained incentives to encourage treasury management groups to locate even more of their activities in Dublin. As Christine Kelly, tax adviser to the IDA, explained to potential clients, the hope was that more corporations could 'benefit from the alignment of business and tax objectives . . . For example, in the treasury sector there are opportunities arising from the potential to convert treasury operations into combined holding and financing operations. The location of both functions in the same jurisdiction offers accounting, tax and legal efficiencies in the redeployment and repatriation of surplus cash around an international group.'

One of the fruits of this strategy was the attraction, in 2009, of Australia's most despised company, the construction materials giant James Hardie. The company's fortune was founded on asbestos mining, leaving it with a huge overhang of compensation claims from sick miners. James Hardie dealt with this embarrassment by skipping off to domicile itself in Holland, leaving two small subsidiaries to deal with the compensation payments. These companies had assets of A$180 million, compared to a likely cost of asbestos-related claims estimated by a special commission of inquiry at A$1.5 billion. The 'singularly unattractive' idea, as the commission put it, was that 'the holding company would make the cheapest provision thought "marketable" in respect of those liabilities so that it could go off to pursue its other more lucrative interests insulated from those liabilities'.

James Hardie's spinning of the truth in relation to this shortfall was referred to by the commission as a 'culture of denial'. The commission remarked that 'for nearly thirty years in this country we have had standards for business communications. Such communications are not to be misleading or deceptive . . . In my opinion they were not here observed.' In 2007, the Australian Securities and Investments Commission commenced civil proceedings against a number of current and former James Hardie directors, and sought declarations that the company had 'made misleading statements and contravened continuous disclosure requirements'.

In 2009, James Hardie decided that it would feel right at home in Ireland. In its statement to shareholders on the proposed move of its HQ to Dublin, it pointed to the irritation that Dutch law imposed 'the requirement for key senior managers to spend substantial time in the Netherlands away from key markets and operations in order to qualify for US/Netherlands tax treaty benefits'. In facilitating global corporate tax avoidance, the Dutch expected those corporations to observe the niceties of actually pretending to be operating from the Netherlands. The Irish required no such pretence. Besides, as the prospectus put it, the move 'increases the company's flexibility by allowing certain types of transactions under Irish law'. As seasoned practitioners of the 'culture of denial', James Hardie would be a fitting addition to the Potemkin village on the Liffey.

That Ireland was still in 2009 the favoured hang-out for ghost headquarters and global corporate refugees was a tribute to its own 'culture of denial'. After the Houldsworth scandals, the government and the regulators carried on as if nothing had happened.

At the IFSC annual lunch in December 2005, the first formal occasion for political comment after Houldsworth's guilty plea, the Minister for Enterprise, Micheál Martin, said nothing about the scandals but instead noted the 'unhappiness in the business sector at the degree and extent of obligations imposed by directors' compliance statement obligations'. He boasted that he was changing these regulations to ensure that the law would be 'less prescriptive about the methods a company uses to review its compliance procedures, and in not requiring review of the compliance statement by an external auditor'.

Even more importantly, Charlie McCreevy, now the EU Internal Markets commissioner, with responsibility for financial regulation, stood firmly by the idea of 'principles based' regulation in which everyone agrees to nice ethical codes (not specific rules) and it is up to company boards (not external supervisors) to enforce them. He told the German-Irish Chamber of Commerce that 'There is a temptation at national level to "gold-plate" rules and regulations, which only serve to impede the market without delivering effective assurances for consumers. This is a temptation we all need to resist . . . What Europe needs is a well-regulated but not over-regulated financial system.'

More starkly still, McCreevy made a speech directly to the Financial Regulator in Dublin in October 2005. He not only made no explicit reference to the scandals at the IFSC but the only possible, oblique nod in their direction was a warning that 'we must resist the temptation to rush to regulate every time an accident occurs'.

He then launched into a paean to the virtues of letting it all hang out and the evils of regulation:

My political philosophy is based on giving people freedom. That includes freedom to make money and freedom
to lose it. Freedom to make mistakes and to learn from
them. Freedom to equip yourself with the knowledge you
need to buy a financial product and freedom to 'buy it on
the blind'. These freedoms have to be exercised within the
framework of laws that are fair and that are proportion-
ate, laws that punish mis-sellers and wrongdoers – and
punish them hard – but not within a framework that is
stifling, disproportionate, or that destroys the motivation
to innovate . . . Many of us in this room are from the
generations that had the luck to grow up before governments got working and lawyers got rich on regulating our
lives. We were part of the 'unregulated generation' – the
generation that has produced some of the best risk takers,
problem solvers, and inventors. We had freedom, failure,
success and responsibility and we learnt how to deal with
them all . . . Don't try to protect everyone from every
possible accident.

McCreevy and many of his listeners were indeed from the
'unregulated generation' that had planted the flag of freedom
from Dublin to the Cayman Islands before boldly going into
the uncharted virtual territories of ghost banks and brass-
plate companies. They had seen plenty of innovation and
invention, as people thought up new ways to evade their
taxes or shift billions through the ether. They had seen plenty of 'mistakes' and 'accidents'. All they lacked was the
slightest ability to learn from them.

In spite of four major scandals involving criminal behaviour (DIRT, Ansbacher, Parmalat and Cologne Re), there was
no sense that the political and regulatory systems ought to

regard the financial industry with a sharp eye and at a cool distance. Socially, culturally and ideologically, there was a shared set of assumptions and values that made it very easy to move from one side of the fence to the other. The borders between politicians and bankers, regulators and regulated became ever more porous.

The Fianna Fáil stalwart and former Minister for Foreign Affairs David Andrews is chairman of the board of AIG Europe, which made political contributions to his son Barry. The Irish Bankers Federation is headed by the former Fianna Fáil general secretary Pat Farrell. Liam O'Reilly went from being chief executive of the Financial Regulator to being a member of the boards of Merrill Lynch International Bank and of Irish Life and Permanent. While holding these banking positions, O'Reilly was still chairman of the Chartered Accountants Regulatory Board. 'Liam's long experience in financial services, public administration and economic and monetary policy in Ireland and at EU level will be invaluable,' Irish Life's chairperson Gillian Bowler explained on his appointment. On joining Merrill Lynch, O'Reilly explained that 'Merrill Lynch asked me to join with good motives. It was to make sure that they were doing things right. I would be like a watchdog for them inside.' His bark seems to have been as gentle as his bite had been when he was a regulator. In February 2009, Merrill Lynch announced that the Dublin-based operation may have had a rogue trader on its books, costing it up to $120 million.

Paddy Teahon, former secretary general of the Department of the Taoiseach, and one of the most influential civil servants of the entire Celtic Tiger period, was also a director of Merrill Lynch's IFSC operation and of the huge property development company Treasury Holdings. Paul Haran, former secretary general of the Department of Enterprise, Trade and Employment, is a director of Bank of Ireland, which paid him €122,000 in 2008 and €119,000 in 2009.

Adrian Byrne, who had raised suspicions about the Ansbacher scam back in the 1970s, and then became head of banking supervision at the Central Bank (and, until 2005, personal adviser to the chief executive of the Financial Regulator) is a director of the IFSC-based West LB Covered Bond Bank Plc. He is also a director of Intrinsic Value Investors Umbrella Fund Plc, an investment fund administered by State Street Fund Services, based at the IFSC. Maurice O'Connell, who was a senior figure at the Department of Finance during the bank scandals of the 1980s and then became the governor of the Central Bank, is a director of Defpa Bank at the IFSC. There is no suggestion that any of these men behaved in any way unethically or that they were ever less than diligent in performing their duties. The point, simply, is that no one moving between the worlds of supervision and active banking was likely to suffer from culture shock.

Perhaps the most vivid illustration of the ease with which regulators could move from one side of the fence to the other is the career of William Slattery, whose prescient warnings about the level of debt in the Irish economy were quoted in Chapter 5. He joined the Central Bank in the late 1970s and was directly responsible for the supervision of the IFSC from its inception in 1987 until 1995. He became deputy head of banking supervision, with hands-on responsibility for the regulation of all the banks and building societies. In 1996, less than a year after he left this position, he joined Deutsche International Ireland, an Irish subsidiary of the German bank, dedicated to servicing hedge funds, derivative funds and other offshore operations. From there, he became head of the Irish division of the US financial services holding company State Street, and of its European Offshore Domiciles division.

Most remarkably, Slattery also chaired, from 2002 to 2005, the bankers' lobby group Financial Services Ireland (FSI). In that role, he was at the forefront of the fight against nasty regulators like William Slattery in his previous incarnation. At the annual dinner of FSI in the opulent Four Seasons Hotel in Ballsbridge in 2003, he complained to his fellow bankers that 'I regret to say that there is a palpable sense of unease within the financial sector in Ireland about what is becoming an over-regulated business environment. There has been a dramatic increase in the regulation of our economy in recent years. In public debate in Ireland, more regulation is regarded as good, and, increasingly, regulation is regarded as a panacea for all sorts of public policy issues . . . I believe that the sheer extent and complexity of regulation in recent years has damaged the competitiveness of the economy. I believe that the expectations of politicians, the media and the public, regarding the beneficial impact of regulation, are exaggerated.'

With such antipathy to regulation even from the former regulator of the IFSC, it is not surprising that Irish-based financial companies played a large part in the global banking crisis that unfolded in 2007 and 2008. Bear Stearns, one of the biggest institutions to collapse in the credit crunch, had two investment funds and six debt securities listed on the Irish Stock Exchange, and it operated three subsidiaries in the IFSC, through a holding company, Bear Stearns Ireland Ltd.

Jim Stewart identified nineteen funds caught up in the subprime crisis and located at the IFSC. Four German banks with funds quoted in Dublin were caught up in the crisis –

Bayern LB, IKB Bank, Sachsen LB and West LB. IKB Bank took losses of €2 billion from an off-balance-sheet conduit called Rhineland Plc with funds quoted in Dublin. The German government had to bail it out to the tune of €7.8 billion. Sachsen bank required emergency funding of €17.3 billion because of 'liquidity difficulties' with its Dublin-based sub-prime funds, with the cute local names of Ormond Quay and Georges Quay. As early as 2004, the German financial regulator had warned its Irish counterpart that these funds were engaging in risky and murky investment practices, including on the US subprime market, but the Irish essentially dis-avowed all responsibility for monitoring them.

Depfa Bank, with Maurice O'Connell on its board, nearly caused its very own catastrophe for the Irish taxpayer. It was, as we have seen, officially an Irish bank, with its global HQ in Dublin. In theory, it was an ultra-safe institution, lending money to public sector clients in the developed world. In practice, it was funding much of this long-term lending with short-term borrowing on the money markets. When those markets dried up after the collapse of Lehman Brothers in September 2008, Depfa teetered towards collapse. It was pure luck (for the Irish) that Depfa had been taken over in September 2007 by the German commercial property lender Hypo Real Estate. Depfa's implosion triggered the collapse of Hypo, ultimately costing the German taxpayer over €100 billion in guarantees and credit lines. If Hypo had not taken over Depfa twelve months before the collapse, the problem would have belonged exclusively to little old Ireland. The havoc that the Bermuda of Europe had created for the rest of the continent would have been wreaked on Depfa's island home.

7

Off-line Ireland

'Zero or very close to it'
– report on the progress of MediaLab Ireland

The first mass-market personal computer was introduced by IBM in 1981. The Apple Mac came along in 1984, followed by Microsoft Windows in 1985. That same year, the first widely sold laptop was launched by Toshiba. The World Wide Web arrived in 1989 and the first web browser in 1993. The first mobile phone with internet connectivity was launched by Nokia in 1996. Yahoo! was founded in 1995 and Google in 1998. Developments of some significance – email, social networking, YouTube, Twitter – flowed from these innovations.

These changes were of some importance in the little world of information technology. They were also of some consequence for Ireland. The country became the premier location worldwide for US investment in information technology. By 2006, Intel had 5,000 employees in Ireland; Dell 4,300; IBM 3,500; Hewlett Packard 2,500; and Microsoft 1,200. By the mid- 2000s, Ireland was the world's leading exporter of computer software and a third of all personal computers sold in Europe were manufactured in the Republic.

Yet, as far as the Irish educational system was concerned, none of this had really happened. In 1980, an optional computer studies module was included in the Leaving Certificate mathematics syllabus. It was 'intended that this would be a first step in the development of computer studies in the post-primary curriculum'. Another optional course for junior cycle students was introduced in 1985. And that was that. As a Department of Education report acknowledged in 2008, 'neither of the computer studies courses has been revised since their introduction, nor has there been any further development of computer studies courses, as such, as part of the curriculum in either the junior or the senior cycle.'

As far as the Irish educational curriculum was concerned, it was still 1980. Computers were huge, mysterious, overheated machines with flashing lights held in vast rooms where boffins in white coats fed them with punch cards and ticker tape. Spooky *Doctor Who*-type music played in the background, barely drowning out the clicks and whirrs. Internet cafes, *Second Life, Halo 3* and illegal downloads were science fiction. It was an educational variant on *Life on Mars* without the car chases or the postmodern irony.

Nowhere was the smugness, indolence and incompetence of Irish governments more obvious than in the yawning chasm between the rhetoric of a high-tech, cutting edge, innovative society and the reality its education system scarcely bothered to acknowledge. The rhetoric was fine: as early as 1999, the government's Information Society Action Plan declared that 'If we are to maintain and build on our economic success of recent years, and ensure that all of society can participate in the Information Society, it is vital that Ireland becomes both an early mover and a global player in the Information Society. Failure to take action could mean that much of the strong economic performance of recent years could be lost.' There was, in the abstract, a consensus that Irish prosperity could not be sustained unless the presence of so many world-class IT companies was used to create a culture in which technological and scientific innovation did not have to be imported.

That knowledge of what had to happen failed to compute. Free-market ideology, the property craze and the stubborn attachment of middle-class aspirations to essentially nine-teenth-century patterns combined to ensure that there was no transformation.

In April 2002, the Taoiseach, Bertie Ahern, signed the pref-ace to a report published by his department called the New Connections Action Plan. He told the nation that the impact of IT on governance was 'bringing about the single most dynamic shift in the public policy environment in the history of the state'. He told us that 'The development of e-govern-ment is also central to shaping how we evolve as an informa-tion society . . . Given its key infrastructural significance, progress with e-government is increasingly seen internation-ally as . . . a key determinant of national competitiveness.'

'Key', 'central', 'single most dynamic' – this is the lan-guage of absolute priorities. A marker was being set down: judge us by how we deal with this stuff. If you actually read the report that followed, however, you would have felt immediately uneasy. It was awash with the kind of jargon and management-speak that is the infallible sign of a chancer: 'there is growing acceptance of the need for a greater internal e-government focus on streamlining back-ground processes, facilitating cross-organisational collabo-ration, continuing to develop an organisational culture with a user-centric focus, and achieving the full benefits from the substantial investments in technology across the public ser-vice.' People who know what they're doing don't take refuge in this kind of babble.

And, of course, Bertie and his mandarins were bluffing.

Setting up a special cabinet committee on the information society, boasting about our 'global leadership position' in high-tech industry and putting e- before every noun that had the misfortune to crawl across a screen were just masks for cluelessness.

Here is a brief summary of just some of the big IT projects sponsored by the government in the Celtic Tiger years.

MediaLab Europe was established by Bertie Ahern as a 'flagship project'. It got €35 million of public money and the state also leased it, for a nominal rent, property that had cost €22.5 million. After four years, an outside review found that its progress towards meeting its objectives of cutting edge high-tech innovation 'appeared to be zero or very close to it'. It was liquidated in 2005.

The Department of Social and Family Affairs set up a computerised Client Identity Service (CIS) in 2000 to manage the PPS number registration system. It didn't recognise 'foreign' names so anyone foolish to have one could be allocated a PPS number that was already in use. Fraudulently obtained PPS numbers could not be deleted, flagged or rendered unusable. More than one PPS number could be allocated to the same person on the same day.

The HRMS computer system installed in the prison service in 2004 was so useless that it was completely abandoned a few months later, though not until after €340,000 had been spent on software licences and €175,000 on consultants.

In 2002, the Department of the Environment ordered 6,315 electronic voting machines at a cost of €51 million. They were tried out in a few constituencies, but proved to be dangerously insecure. Simply keeping them in storage cost close to €1 million a year, until they were finally scrapped in 2009. Not even Florida would take them.

The introduction of penalty points for dangerous driving in October 2002 saved lives. But the positive effect gradually faded as it became clear to drivers that the Garda did not have a computer system that could handle the work. Ireland's 'global leadership position' in IT meant that the police were keeping the records by writing them down in ledgers like Dickensian clerks.

The Garda PULSE computer system, which cost €61 million, was so bad that in many cases gardaí again reverted to writing charge sheets by hand.

In public health administration, use of both the Personnel, Payroll and Related Systems (PPARS) scheme, which has cost €180 million so far in spite of an initial budget of €8.8 million, and the FISP financial information system, which had cost at least €30 million, had to be suspended in 2006, since neither of them could do the job it was supposed to do.

A computerised integrated ticketing system for Dublin's various modes of public transport was first announced by the government in November 2000. At the time of writing, the most optimistic expectations were that it might happen at the end of 2009.

As for e-government, a 2008 report by the Comptroller and Auditor General found that although an estimated €420 million (not including the very considerable cost of internal staff) had been spent on developing online services between 2000 and 2005, Ireland had completely failed to become a world leader in the field: 'While Ireland has some on-line transaction services that compare favourably with what has been achieved elsewhere, an EU-wide benchmark survey indicates that it has achieved the highest level of on-line service in only ten of 22 key public services for individual and business users . . . Overall, Ireland's position is around the average for EU member states and some states are delivering a significantly higher level of on-line service.' For an economy that needed to be at the cutting edge, being average was a significant failure.

All of this points to an obvious conclusion – that almost no one in government, and relatively few in the civil service, had any real understanding of information technology. When it came to discussing either IT or science in general, ministers could generally do no more than parrot the gobbledygook they had been fed by consultants and advisers. When in December 2008, Mary Coughlan, Minister for Enterprise, set up an EFG on the implementation of the SSTI (that is, an Enterprise Feedback Group on the government's Strategy for Science, Technology and Innovation), it was not easy to be optimistic about the government's plan 'for Ireland to become a world-class knowledge economy by 2013'.

The bullshit factor was most evident in two areas – broadband and education.

Broadband was one of the very few areas in which the government had a very clear goal, to be achieved within a very specific time-frame. In March 2002, Bertie Ahern's New Connections document stated that 'Government wants to see the widespread availability of open-access, affordable, always-on broadband infrastructure and services for businesses and citizens throughout the state within three years . . . We wish to see Ireland within the top decile of OECD countries for broadband connectivity within three years.' This could hardly have been clearer – by March 2005, Ireland would be one of the top ten countries in the developed world. Broadband would be reasonably cheap and it would be available throughout the state. Ireland would also become the first European country to have video-quality broadband speeds (5 Mbps or higher) widely available.

This was a fairly tough task to achieve in three years, but getting it done was both necessary and possible. It was an absolute necessity because otherwise all the talk about being on the leading edge of global technology was just so much waffle. It was possible because other small, geographically peripheral countries like Finland, Iceland, Denmark and South Korea were managing it. Indeed, it was precisely small, peripheral countries that had most to gain.

And, fortunately, the government had the vehicle with which to achieve its goals: the state telecommunications company Eircom, which owned the telephone infrastructure. Or rather, it used to have. For in one of the most breathtaking follies of the Celtic Tiger era, the government had flogged off Eircom precisely at the time when it was setting its goals of making Ireland a world-leading information society. For purely ideological reasons, the state sold off its controlling majority stake in Eircom in 1999 for €4.1 billion. Hence the small, scarcely noticed caveat after the announcement in 2002 that Ireland would be one of the ten most connected societies in the world: 'The state's role in this area is confined to provision of seed capital.' Ireland's IT miracle was to be a purely private affair. The market would miraculously provide the cheap, universal service that was a key goal of national strategy.

The privatisation of Eircom was a fiasco almost from the start. It was an attempt to whip up the fervour for 'popular capitalism' that Margaret Thatcher had generated in the UK in the 1980s. It worked: 575,000 people bought shares in the initial public offering. Two and a half years later, almost all of them had lost 30 per cent of their investment when the company was sold off to American venture capitalists (the Valentia consortium) and taken off the stock exchange.

This was just the prelude to a long-running farce as Eircom was passed around among global venture capitalists like a joint at a student party. Each one inhaled the assets before passing it on. Having been taken off the market in 2001 by the Valentia consortium, it floated again in 2004, and was then acquired by Australian bank Babcock Brown in 2006. At each stage, Eircom was loaded with the debt borrowed in order to acquire it – it had debts of €3.4 billion at the end of 2008. In 2009, Eircom was up for sale again, this time to a Singapore-based consortium, setting up its fifth change of ownership in under ten years. In this game of pass-the-parcel, the only object has been to squeeze as much short-term profit out of the company as possible. Long-term investment of the kind needed to create a world-class IT infrastructure has been the last thing on anyone's mind.

This whole process was very good for a small number of people. It didn't take long for popular capitalism to revert to the good old-fashioned unpopular variety. The members of the Valentia consortium who swooped on Eircom in 2001 made fortunes without doing much beyond loading it with debt. Tony O'Reilly made a clear profit of €35 million; the George Soros Fund raked in €177 million and Providence Equity made €443 million. The employee share ownership trust, which had leveraged trade union power into an astonishingly lucrative deal for its members, made €177 million. In total, on this one change of ownership alone, there were profits of nearly a billion euro. This was money that should have been invested in creating the promised broadband infrastructure.

Needless to say, with the main player in the Irish fixed-line telecommunications market too busy servicing the needs of global venture capitalists, Ireland did not become one of the top ten countries in this field in 2005. Or in any year thereafter. It became instead a place where most people were deeply grateful for a 1 Mb connection and a third of the country had no access to broadband at all.

As of December 2008, Ireland was twenty-first of thirty OECD countries for the number of broadband subscribers per 100 inhabitants, twenty-fifth for the geographical penetration of broadband services and thirty-first of thirty-five for the average advertised download speed. The fastest speed available from the main operator (Eircom) was the fourth slowest in the OECD – over twelve times slower than in France or Finland. As for the goal of being the first country in Europe to have widely available 5 Mbps broadband, the reality is that Ireland may well be the last.

This failure had its roots in ideologically induced stupidity. The €4.1 billion it would have cost the state to directly provide a 5 Mbps service for most of the country was less than the €6 billion that the National Pension Reserve Fund, into which the money from the sale of Eircom was put, lost on international stock exchanges in 2008. But it was more important to pursue the delusion that the market would provide vital national infrastructure than to actually achieve a crucial transformation.

Beyond this idiocy, however, there was a larger question of cultural change. Could Ireland, which had an abundance of creativity in the arts, develop a similarly strong technological imagination? Could the kind of leading-edge technological know-how that had been imported with transnational corporations become an organic aspect of Irish culture? The key to this obviously lay in education. But the government had better things to spend its technology budgets on, like useless e-voting machines and prestige IT projects that couldn't even crunch the fabulous numbers of euros they were costing.

Some of this stuff was very simple: giving kids access to computers in schools, for example. There is one computer for every nine pupils in Irish primary schools and one for every seven in secondary schools; the leading countries have a ratio of one to three or four. Even this makes things look better than they are. A third of the stock of computers in primary schools, and a fifth at post-primary level, is more than six years old and 'not capable of running much modern software'. Most schools at every level don't have a sufficient budget to maintain the computers and digital equipment they do have, so much of it is out of order much of the time.

In England, two-thirds of primary schools and almost all secondary schools use interactive whiteboards in the classroom; the figures in Ireland are 5 per cent and 2 per cent respectively. Fewer than a third of Irish primary teachers, and a quarter of secondary teachers, rate their own ability to use IT in the classroom as 'intermediate' or above. Department of Education inspectors saw IT being used in just 22 per cent of lessons in primary schools and rated the use of IT in the classroom as 'competent or optimal' in just a quarter of cases.

Not surprisingly, the levels of accomplishment in computer skills are quite low. The inspectors noted that 'many fifth-class students in primary schools do not have the competence to complete basic tasks on the computer. While most students reported being able to perform many of the most basic computer tasks, such as turning a computer on and off and opening or saving a file, more than 30 per cent reported that they were not able to print a document or to go on the internet by themselves. Almost half reported not being able to create a document by themselves.' Eighty-eight per cent did not know how to send an attachment with an e-mail. And even after five years of post-primary education, most students were found to need help with tasks like moving files or sending e-mails.

Given all of this, it is hardly mysterious that Ireland failed completely to create a culture in which science and technology are really valued. Just 16 per cent of students took higher level mathematics in the Leaving Certificate in 2009, just 10 per cent sat higher level chemistry and just 8 per cent attempted higher level physics. Interest in maths seems to have actually declined during the high-tech boom years. In 1992, when the higher level syllabus was introduced, it was expected that 20 to 25 per cent of students would take the exam. In 2001, the figure was 18 per cent. By 2009, it was 16 per cent. In 2005, the Department of Education's chief examiner complained of 'a noticeable slippage, over a short period of time, in both the quality of work and the capacity of candidates to engage with problems that were not of a routine nature'. If maths is the language of the twenty-first century knowledge economy, the Irish were becoming steadily less articulate.

This was not some kind of genetic quirk. Ireland was perfectly capable of producing world-class mathematics graduates and of turning maths-based technologies into world-class companies. One of them, Havok, spun out of a Trinity College Dublin campus company and later bought by Intel for $100 million, is probably the global leader in the application of physics to video games and movies, powering the effects in everything from *Halo* and *Guitar Hero* to *The Matrix* and *Charlie and the Chocolate Factory*. But the appalling state of broadband development and the small numbers of maths graduates made it difficult for such companies to remain in Ireland. Havok's managing director David O'Meara warned in April 2009 that 'the Irish education system is at best only average by Western standards and is not producing the calibre of graduate we want in quality and quantity . . . You would think that the development centre for the next generation of Havok's software would be in Dublin. But 10 years into the company's history and we are looking at other major development centres, where we have operations, in Munich and San Francisco.'

Behind this disastrous failure to create a sustainable and indigenous high-tech culture were two big questions. What do you want to be? And what do you do with your money? Weirdly, the answer to both questions was to be found, not in the globalised Ireland of the Celtic Tiger years but in the nineteenth century. The profound conservatism of Irish society meant that in crucial ways fundamental attitudes had remained frozen throughout a period of apparently total change. Because Ireland had 'imported' its development rather than going through a complete process of democratic modernisation, impulses from another era continued to have a shaping influence on Irish society.

The answer to the question 'what do I want to be?' was largely the same as it was for the educated and aspirant Catholic middle-class in the nineteenth century – a doctor or a lawyer. (It is true, of course, that the old version might also have included a priest or a nun and the new one might have included a pharmacist, a vet or a media star.) The prestige of the higher professions – and the financial rewards attached to them – remained glitteringly intact. Their lustre completely outshone science, maths or technology.

This was clear from the relative difficulty of gaining a university place in these fields. Under the Irish system, the number of points acquired from Leaving Certificate results that were required to gain entry to a particular course gave a brutally frank measure of how much certain kinds of knowledge mattered. The picture was sobering – medicine and law matter an awful lot, science hardly at all. In 2009, for example, the number of points required to study electronic engineering at the largest university, University College Dublin, was 350. Computer science was 370. General science was 385. Law was 470. Medicine was the equivalent of 580.

The lack of interest in computing was stunning. There was a drop of 70 per cent in applications for computing degrees between 2001 and 2003. The numbers graduating in computing applications from Dublin City University, for example, dropped from 224 in 2005 to just 74 in 2008. Many science and technology courses struggled to fill their places. As a result, more than half of postgraduate places in computer-related courses were filled by students from outside Ireland. Software companies in Ireland were similarly unable to fill the jobs they had on offer – half of new recruits were hired from abroad.

Some of this had to do with gender – young women, who increasingly dominated entry to third-level education, were particularly reluctant to think about careers in IT. And some of it had to do with class. The Irish professional classes were extremely efficient at reproducing themselves. In 2008–9, almost half of medical students and over one-third of law students in Irish universities came from professional family backgrounds. While higher professionals (doctors, solicitors, barristers, engineers, pharmacists, etc.) account for just 5 per cent of the Irish population, their children account for close to one-third of students on courses oriented towards the professions: 32 per cent of first years in medicine, 27 per cent in veterinary medicine, 23 per cent in law and 19 per cent in pharmacy. (By contrast, not a single student entering university courses in pharmacy or medicine in 2008–9 came from an unskilled manual background.) As the chief executive of the Higher Education Authority put it, 'The socioeconomic profile on these courses has changed very little over the past decade.' There was, in fact, a conservative cycle that proved much more powerful than the surface changes in the Irish economy: the professionals dominated the university system and they wanted their children to be professionals. Family cultures, many of them formed with the rise of the Catholic middle-class in the nineteenth century, remained substantially intact.

The other nineteenth-century impulse was land. What do you do with your money? You put it in property. Most of the wealth generated by the Celtic Tiger was new money. But when it came to spending it, there was a very old formula: bricks, mortar (or at the higher end, steel and concrete) and the land they stand on.

When Bertie Ahern said that the developers and builders who gathered in the party tent at the Galway races to pay homage (and cash) to Fianna Fáil were Ireland's wealth creators, he summed up the underlying belief that real money was made by real men by putting up real buildings. Whatever lip service was paid to the notions of innovation and the knowledge economy, these quirks never had any visceral grasp on the governing mind. All the signals that were sent out, not least through tax breaks, were that property was the proper place for money.

Between 2000 and 2008, Irish venture capital firms invested

€1.2 billion in Irish small and medium enterprises. A great deal of this was in high-tech companies, though only around a third of it was in start-up or young enterprises. To put this €1.2 billion in context, it is exactly the same as the sum spent by Irish investors buying properties in London in the first six months of 2008, a period when property investment was in sharp decline. Irish individuals and companies made €41 billion in capital gains from investments in land, property and equities in the three years between 2004 and 2007. In a slightly longer period (between 2001 and 2006) Irish people invested €41 billion in commercial property at home and abroad. In 2006 and 2007 alone, the Irish invested almost €20 billion in foreign property.

The sheer scale of this rush to buy buildings in foreign climes is remarkable. In 2007, the second biggest slice (after the UK) of money invested in the entire European property market was Irish. The Irish spent nearly €14 billion that year. The French spent €11 billion and the Dutch €8 billion.

When the property crash came, Irish people were rather surprised to learn that of the €90 billion in development loans that were dragging down the Irish banking system, €25 billion related to property in the UK and €3 billion in the US. (An unknown, but probably very substantial, amount was related to continental Europe – €2.6 billion was invested from Ireland in France and Germany in 2007 alone.)

In truth, this outflow of money (which came from moguls buying office blocks, barristers buying villas in Portugal or Florida and middle-class investors buying apartments in Bulgaria) combined two primeval instincts: put money into property and get it out of the country. While the ideological justification for the government's cosseting of the rich was that their money would trickle downwards into the Irish economy, much of it actually flooded out of Ireland. The total stock of foreign portfolio asset securities held by Irish residents at the end of 2007 amounted to €1,338 billion – that's €1.3 trillion, about the same as the projected US budget deficit at the end of 2009. While much was always made (rightly) of US investment in Ireland, it was easily forgotten that there was also a powerful flow in the other direction. Little Ireland is now the tenth largest investor in the United States – not in relative but in absolute terms. In 2004, for the first time, outflows of foreign direct investment *from* Ireland exceeded inflows *into* Ireland. The number of Americans employed by Irish companies in the US is about 75 per cent of the number of Irish people employed in Ireland by US companies.

The reluctance to invest in innovative Irish companies, the complete failure to get within a sniff of the world-class broadband infrastructure that was supposed to be a national priority, and the failure to create through the education system an organic technological culture were huge cracks in the facade of high-tech Ireland. They were indirect but deeply damaging effects of the cronyism, lack of ambition and idolatry of raw money that dominated the political system. While money, energy, ingenuity and political support were stoking the property boom, Ireland's response to the technological forces that had helped to create the Celtic Tiger were increasingly less reminiscent of Silicon Valley and more of *The IT Crowd*.

8

Unknown Knowns

'Those who have shaped our modern, thriving nation can
escape as a little reward once in a while, without ever losing touch
with home' – brochure for the Island of Ireland

'The "Island of Ireland" is strategically located at the centre
of "The World".' As a statement of the self-absorption and
grandiose delusions of Celtic Tiger Ireland, this one would
take some beating. But it is intended literally. The 'Island of
Ireland' is not the island of Ireland. 'The World' is not the
world. The island is part of a man-made archipelago off the
coast of Dubai, 300 artificial platforms in the Arabian Gulf,
surrounded by an oval breakwater shaped to form the map
of the world.

On the 225,000-square-foot Island of Ireland, owned by a
consortium led by the Galway-based property developer
John O'Dolan, the plan was to have just a hint of 'the archi-
tecture of Ireland through the ages'. In case potential
investors might be put off by the thought of damp thatched
cottages festering in the rain or dreary bungalows on
windswept hills, the promotional brochure stressed that this
would mostly consist of a 'landscaped courtyard area, evok-
ing the wide Georgian squares of Dublin'. For older property developers, there would presumably be a warm glow of
nostalgia for the Georgian squares that they and their men-
tors had done their best to obliterate in the 1960s and 1970s.

The plan, aptly enough, was endorsed on the scheme's
website by the serving Taoiseach Bertie Ahern who evoked

'substantial Irish achievement across a wide range of human endeavours' and expressed the hope that the 'Island of Ireland' would be 'seen as symbolic of the best of those achievements and reflect the confidence and vision of Irish people in the new millennium'. These achievements, the brochure made clear, were those of the millionaires who had made Ireland what it was and who now deserved a literal place in the sun: 'We had a vision . . . to bring a little piece of Ireland to the sun. To create a luxury hotel resort to which those who have shaped our modern, thriving nation can escape as a little reward once in a while, without ever losing touch with home.'

The pitch was perfectly tuned. The great men who 'shaped our modern, thriving nation' could have their Irish pride in villas with 'more than just a hint of Irishness to them', but they would not actually have to be in Ireland – a particular advantage for those among them who were tax fugitives. This would be the perfect Ireland, with a vague sense of 'history' in its mock-Georgian squares but no politics, with a simulacrum of Irish conviviality ('bars that will remind you of home') without the bother of an unruly plebeian populace (this is 'the most exclusive real-estate development on the planet'). It would also be the perfect form of globalisation – a world with Ireland at its centre, like Jerusalem in medieval maps. The multi-millionaire's solipsism and self-regard would mesh seamlessly with the fantasy of a Hibernocentric universe: 'The World can actually revolve around you!'

The Island of Ireland in Dubai was the incarnation of a fantasy that had hovered around the collective imagination of Ireland's elite for a long time. In the late 1980s and early 1990s, Irish intellectuals revived the idea of the Fifth Province (Mary Robinson evoked it in her inaugural speech as president in 1990). They meant a place of art, ideas and ideals. But the real fifth province of the Irish imagination was a sunny Ireland, washed by a bluer, warmer ocean, where there were no taxes, no history and no social obligations.

In Charles Haughey's era this fifth province was Grand Cayman island, where money frolicked under palm trees, free from the predations of the taxman and the prying eyes of those who wondered about its origins. In Bertie Ahern's era, it was Bermuda, whose tax-haven status Ireland hoped to emulate. It was not for nothing that while English critics referred to the Irish Financial Services Centre in Dublin as 'Liechtenstein on the Liffey', the Industrial Development Authority preferred, as we have seen, to aspire to be 'the Bermuda of Europe'. The Island of Ireland in Dubai brought these two notions together – a sunny island that was far away but still, somehow, 'home'.

Even when this fantasy had to be actually brought home to the process of making money from property development in dark, rainy Ireland, it retained its grip. In the Celtic Tiger era of property development, Ireland was always subtropical. As the property editor of the *Irish Times,* Orna Mulcahy, noted of one of the iconic (doubly iconic in being unbuilt) developments of the boom years, Seán Dunne's would-be 'new Knightsbridge' in Ballsbridge:

> I dug out the architects' drawings from the bottom of
> a heap under my desk and yes, there it was: sunshine,
> flooding the imagined plazas and courtyards and
> bouncing off the glass of towering apartment blocks.
> Pert-breasted women strolling around in T-shirts and
> sunglasses. Even the underground shopping mall
> appeared to have an abundance of sunlight spilling in

via a mini Eden project jutting up at ground level, filled with palms, orchids and cacti. The central piazza, with 14- and 15-storey buildings all around, had the baked ochre look of a Las Vegas resort slumbering in 100 degree heat, with office windows above flung open . . . On the property developer's compass, you see, there is no north. Invariably, their computer-generated plans for housing or office schemes are forever drenched in sunshine, no matter what the aspect. High noon-type shadows are cast by computer-generated people . . . the vast majority of balconies built during the boom faced south – even the many that actually looked due north and enjoyed direct sunlight about once a year, Newgrange-style, on June 21st at four in the morning.

In other countries, global warming is a threat. In Ireland it is a fantasy. The sun-drenched country of the developers' plans actually became the place in which much of the population took up mental residence. During the boom years, people under forty stopped wearing overcoats, even in the dismal winter. The Atlantic wind that stabbed through a flimsy jacket and T-shirt or turned the bare legs of short-skirted girls blue was really a gentle zephyr. Cafes and restaurants began to colonise the footpaths outside their doors for the alfresco dining appropriate to the rain-free, sunlit climate.

There was, moreover, a physical extrusion of Ireland to the world's sunspots as Irish people invested enormous sums in property abroad. Of the €50-plus billion of Irish money spent on buying foreign property, much of the large-scale commercial investment was in the UK or the US. But a substantial amount was spent on acquiring either second homes or investment properties in the Mediterranean, the Adriatic or even further afield. No location was too exotic, especially if it was an island and sunny. At the height of the boom a not untypical report in the property pages of the *Irish Times* stated that 'Cape Verde Development, a company started by Tom Sheehy, a Clonakilty-based property fit-out specialist and backed mainly by Cork and Limerick business people, sold 200 units of its 449-unit scheme off plans when it launched a few weeks ago, most of them to Irish buyers'. It is questionable whether most of those buyers had never even heard of the Cape Verde islands five years previously.

Foreign property replaced emigration as the source of the Elsewheres that had long been part of the Irish imagination. The little Irelands of Brixton or Boston were now the little islands in the sun.

This imaginative displacement was part of the larger confusion of space that came with Ireland's experience of extreme and rapid globalisation. The question of whether Ireland was a balmy subtropical paradise or a wet, wind-lashed rock on the eastern Atlantic was a subset of a larger question – what continent was Ireland in anyway? That in turn was part of a wider problem – the uncertainties of both space and time that made it hard for Irish people to be quite sure where they were living, and when.

The question of which continent Ireland belonged in was famously posed by Mary Harney when she told the American Bar Association in 2000 that 'History and geography have placed Ireland in a very special position between America and Europe . . . Geographically we are closer to Berlin than Boston. Spiritually we are probably a lot closer to Boston than Berlin.' This idea of Ireland as a liminal space, between one continent and another, its proximity to continental Europe a mere factual detail, was of course highly political. It was intended to identify Ireland as an outpost of American values at the physical and political margin of European ideas. Ireland was really a part of the 'Anglo-Saxon' economy, sharing the thirst of the US and the UK for frantic consumption, property bubbles, free-range banking and the elevation of the private sector above all public purposes.

Harney, to her credit, was quite explicit about this. In that speech, she defined 'the European way as being built on a strong concern for social harmony and social inclusion, with governments being prepared to intervene strongly through the tax and regulatory systems to achieve their desired outcomes'. She contrasted this with the 'American way . . . built on the rugged individualism of the original frontiersmen, an economic model that is heavily based on enterprise and incentive, on individual effort and with limited government intervention'. Ireland, she said, 'sailed closer to the American shore than the European one'. In this tectonic shifting of continental plates, Harney was assuring her audience that Celtic Tiger Ireland was not much interested in 'social harmony and social inclusion' or in governments that use taxation and regulation to limit the inequalities and instabilities of the market. It was interested in those mythically rugged values of the American frontier. This was perhaps just as well, since, in line with Harney's ambitions, Ireland would indeed go on to develop quite a line in cowboy economics and earn the title of the 'Wild West of European finance'.

Yet Harney's figurative shifting of Ireland a few thousand miles to the west was not seen to be absurd. This was partly because of the close historical ties between Ireland and the US and the large scale of American investment in Ireland. But it was also because the Irish sense of belonging in Europe turned out to be much weaker than it had seemed. The EU had been a crucial part of Irish identity between the 1970s and 1990s when it had been the form in which Irish modernity sold itself to a rural and conservative population. It has, paradoxically, vindicated Irish nationalism by finally breaking the dependence of the Irish economy on trade with Britain. It was not surprising that enthusiasm for the European project was particularly high in Ireland.

Yet, as it turned out, it was also particularly shallow. Linguistically, for example, Ireland remained a relentlessly monoglot subset of the English-speaking world. For all the talk of globalisation and cultural complexity, the Irish were stubbornly attached to English as their sole means of communication. In fact the Irish were more loyal to English than the English: 66 per cent of the Irish population speaks only English, compared to 62 per cent of Brits. By contrast, just a third of Germans speak only German.

On the political level, there was an obvious contradiction between the message coming from government that the Irish were more American than European on the one side and, on the other, the message from that same government that the Irish should vote for treaties enhancing and expanding the EU. The Nice Treaty was defeated in a referendum in 2001. Though it was subsequently passed in a re-run in 2002, the defeat prefigured the initial rejection of the Lisbon Treaty by Irish voters in 2008. The underlying scepticism about where Ireland belonged, largely created by the government itself, could not be turned on and off at will. The Celtic Tiger's tendency to snap at the European hand that had fed it in its infancy was encouraged by the same politicians who, when it suited them, insisted that the Irish should be good Europeans.

These confusions in the big picture were also felt at the level of everyday life. If Ireland was metaphorically wandering all over the map of the world, the Irish were literally wandering all over the map of Ireland. Rampant, badly planned development destroyed a coherent sense of place. A vast amount of effort in the late 1990s was put into the development of a National Spatial Strategy, under which regional 'gateways' and 'hubs' would develop a critical mass of population and employment and become sustainable urban centres. It was not simply ignored but actively destroyed by the government. When Charlie McCreevy announced in 2003 a plan to 'decentralise' 10,000 civil and public sector employees from Dublin to the regions, three-quarters of them were to be sent to towns that were not planned for growth under the strategy. It was a clear signal that the whole idea of organising space in a rational way was being abandoned. In 2007, five years after the strategy was supposedly implemented, the president of the Irish Planning Institute, Henk van der Kamp, pointed out that population growth in many counties with 'gateways' or 'hubs' was actually much lower than that in counties without them. In other words, the spatial strategy was completely meaningless.

The effects were felt both in the cities and in small towns and villages. On the one hand, rising house prices in the cities forced would-be home owners out into new commuter belts. Just 4 per cent of the growth in the Irish population between 2002 and 2006 took place in the five main cities combined. The result, especially in relation to Dublin, was a vast expansion of the effective area of the city, in terms of the places where those working within it had their homes. Large swathes of Wicklow, Wexford, Meath, Louth, Westmeath, Carlow, Offaly, even Cavan and Monaghan, became parts of outer Dublin. The very concept of Dublin became extraordinarily diffuse. As early as 2001, the president of the Royal

Institute of Architects in Ireland, Tony Reddy, pointed out that Greater Dublin 'could occupy an area the size of Los Angeles by 2010', even though it would have just a quarter of the American city's population.

In planning terms, this was an outstanding achievement and an example to the world. The European Environment Agency, advising the new Central and Eastern European member states of the EU, pointed to Dublin as the 'worst case scenario' for the handling of growth.

On the other side of this equation, builders, aided by complaisant local authorities, slapped up huge numbers of houses, usually in identikit suburban estates, as appendages to old villages. Many of these villages were simply swamped. Between 1996 and 2006, the number of households in Stamullen increased by 726 per cent; in Ratoath by 651 per cent; in Sallins by 417 per cent, and in Kinnegad by 379 per cent. Even a village like Virginia in Cavan, all of 83 kilometres from Dublin, grew by 124 per cent. With both men and women having to work in Dublin to pay what were still very high mortgages (and to pay for the cars that were now an absolute necessity: 90 per cent of households in commuter counties like Meath and Kildare had at least one car), maintaining a strong sense of place was always going to be a struggle.

Even within the core of a city like Dublin, new apartment complexes often lacked any real sense of connection to the old working-class areas in which they merely happened to have been built. Mary Benson, in a study of the inner-city district of Ringsend, just two kilometres from the city centre, found that those living in new apartments tended to have a very weak sense of place: 'For these residents, Ringsend does not hold any intimate meaning. They do not involve themselves in any meaningful way at a local level. Their social networks are located in specific places away from Ringsend rather than being anchored locally . . . Although they share spatial proximity, there is little evidence of spatial association.'

Just as the Irish relationship to space was being confused by all of these forces, something similar was happening in relation to time. This too happened on both a global and an intimate level.

The Irish boom coincided with not just one 'end of history' but four. There was the general Western illusion that, after the fall of the Berlin Wall, 'history' was over and the American model of free-market democracy would be established as the universal norm. There was the complementary illusion that the historical cycles of capitalism had been ended by the sheer brilliance of the masters of the universe. Gordon Brown was making this claim as early as 1997, but it was a commonplace, especially in the Anglo-Saxon economic world of which Ireland was a part. And there was a specifically Irish 'end of history'. Two of the great continuities of Ireland since the eighteenth century – mass emigration and political violence – seemed, by the late 1990s, to be definitively over.

Together these forces fed a feeling that the past had little relevance to the new era and that it should be, quite literally, obliterated. On a visit to Shanghai, Bertie Ahern sighed with envy at the power of the city's mayor to bulldoze everything in his way: 'Naturally enough I would like to have the power of the mayor that when he decides he wants to do a highway and, if he wants to bypass an area, he just goes straight up and over.'

This fantasy of absolute power over the landscape and its awkward remnants of history was symbolised in the crassest, but perhaps the most characteristic, action of the boom years: the driving of a motorway through the Tara/Skryne valley in County Meath. The Hill of Tara and its surrounding valleys are an ancient sacred landscape, with at least seventy major archaeological monuments, ranging from a Neolithic passage tomb to Iron Age ceremonial earthworks, in and around the hill itself. Because of the spread of commuter dormitories into north Meath and Cavan, it was deemed necessary to build a motorway. The planners and Fianna Fáil seemed to take a perverse pleasure in rejecting alternative routes and insisting that the motorway should go through the Tara valley. The sheer glee with which this was done was a symptom of a deeply neurotic kind of temporal arrogance. Nothing mattered except now.

Paradoxically, this obliteration of a sense of historical time also suggested that the future would be pretty much like the present. The operative tense in the grammar of Ireland's boom was the present continuous. The idea of the future as a different time, with its own imperatives, was largely absent from the Tiger mentality. Sustainability – a concept that incorporates a sense of the future into the present – was the great unthinkable. Thus the utter contempt for planning and environmental considerations expressed in Bertie Ahern's irritated complaint in 2003 that every big infrastructural project had to 'go through eight hoops, through all environmental, planning and blah blah blah, and every blah costs a few hundred million', and his loftily surreal dismissal of all objections to motorway routes as being about 'swans, snails and people hanging out of trees'.

The non-existence of the future meant that it was okay to

build huge numbers of one-off houses in the countryside where the inhabitants were assumed to be ageless – otherwise it might have seemed wise to think about issues like isolation and immobility that might arise when they got old. It also underpinned the decision, in the age of global warming and peak oil, to create a completely car-dependent society. With very limited fossil fuel resources of its own, and a share of energy from renewable sources that was less than half the OECD average, Ireland became one of the highest per capita carbon emitters in the world. Ireland's total energy consumption increased by 83 per cent from 1990 to 2007 – a bad enough record. But transport energy use increased by 181 per cent. The future that Ireland was imagining was an American motopia of the 1950s in which petrol was dirt cheap, guilt-free and infinitely available.

The consequences of this inability to imagine the future were not at all abstract. Since the present was one in which property prices were constantly rising and the historical experiences of boom and bust had been rendered irrelevant, there was no point in listening to those who droned on about what had happened before. To insist that all known housing bubbles had always burst was to miss the point that this was a new time with its own new laws of perpetual motion.

The other paradox, though, was that this apparent reassurance that the vicissitudes of history had been disarmed did not create a sense of calm but, on the contrary, generated hysteria. Time speeded up to a frenzy and slowed down to a enervating grind.

The process of speeding up was a function both of work and of the property market. The pressures of highly productive workplaces and of juggling paid employment with childcare made a nonsense of the old Bord Fáilte image of Ireland as a place with a relaxed pace of life. In a 2006 study from the Economic and Social Research Institute, 57 per cent of working people and 62 per cent of dual-earner couples reported feeling rushed or stressed on weekdays. Even simple tasks that allowed for a degree of dawdling were speeded up: the proportion of children walking to school was cut in half in the boom years.

Meanwhile, in their book *The Builders*, Kathy Sheridan and Frank McDonald quoted one property industry insider on the shift in the idea of a 'phase' in relation to construction and sale of housing estates: 'Before the boom, it used to be Phase 1 this year and Phase 2 the next; now there was a day between them if that.' Builders would set a price, sell a lot of houses quickly and then decide that the price was too cheap. 'What happens then is that you call the next bunch of exact same houses "Phase 2", and the price is hiked maybe 15 per cent. And that could all happen in a few days or in an afternoon.'

In the property bubble, the clock was always ticking loudly – time really was money as prices rose by the day and the pressure to buy something, *anything*, right now became irresistible. Yet partly as a result of that same property mania, much of life moved at a teeth-grindingly slow pace. In the 2002, the main opposition party Fine Gael was much mocked for an ad campaign suggesting that the Celtic Tiger was really a Celtic Snail. The imagery was hopelessly out of tune with the popular mood, but it was not inaccurate.

The poor level of investment in public transport and the consequent dependence on cars made Ireland into the traffic jam capital of the world. Seven out of ten Irish workers were travelling to their jobs by car, and the average distance was nearly 16 kilometres. By 2006, there were 1.2 million cars on the road for a population of 4.2 million – more than one car for every four people, including children. The number of people travelling to work by car increased by nearly a quarter between 2002 and 2006. The results were predictable.

A Small Firms Association study, published in 2001, found that the time taken for a small packet of goods to travel five kilometres in Dublin – 57 minutes – was effectively the longest in the world. This journey time compared to 13 minutes in London, nine in Singapore, and 37 in Mumbai. The only city in the survey to be slower was Calcutta, where most business deliveries were still made on foot. For the same reasons, the average speed of buses in Dublin dropped steadily as the property boom gathered pace. In 2001, it was 15 kilometres an hour, compared to an international average of 20. In 2003, it dropped to 13.5 and in 2005 it was 12.9. In a society that was always telling people they had to move fast, moving very slowly was an increasingly common experience. Waiting – in a car at the infamous Red Cow roundabout on the M50 into Dublin, on a very long list for hospital treatment, in a serpentine queue at the overcrowded Dublin airport – was one of the characteristic modes of life in a frantically fast society.

Perhaps the most confusing thing about the Irish sense of time was that its grand narrative refused to go in a straight line. For what the Irish in Ireland were experiencing as new – rapid urbanisation, multiculturalism, the need to make one's way in a polyglot and physically unfamiliar society – was a recapitulation of the experiences of their own ancestors when they emigrated from rural farms to huge metropolitan centres in the US or Britain. The diasporic life was now lived at home – a logical outcome of the economic reversal in which, instead of Irish labour moving towards American capital, American capital had moved towards Irish labour. The sense of estrangement felt by generations of emigrants could now be felt without actually going anywhere.

These changes in, and confusions of, the Irish relationship to space and time had a profound cumulative effect. They made it difficult for Irish society to develop a coherent image of itself. The place was hard to grasp.

What made it even more so was, paradoxically, one of the great strengths of Irish culture: its capacity for double-think. For a range of reasons – the simultaneous existence of paganism and Christianity, the ambiguous relationship of indigenous society to a colonial power, the long experience of emigration – Irish culture developed a particularly strong capacity for operating simultaneously within different mental frameworks. This is one of the reasons for the rich inventiveness of Irish artistic life and for much of the humour, teasing and wordplay that enliven social interaction. Irish double-think is wonderfully summed up by the old woman in the 1930s who, asked by Seán O'Faoláin if she believed in the little people, replied, 'I do not, sir, but they're there.'

Yet this same capacity to be in two minds has also been at work in many of the most shameful aspects of Irish society. Hypocrisy, in which Irish life abounds, is one of its forms: double-think is closely allied to double standards. So too is the extraordinary capacity of the society to both know and not know things simultaneously. Irish people knew very well that the appalling system of Church-run industrial schools existed in order to inflict pain and punishment on children, yet there was genuine shock and disturbance when the systemic abuse was revealed in the 1990s and confirmed in 2009 in the relentless and devastating report of the Ryan inquiry. In Ireland, there was a refinement on Donald Rumsfeld's infamous ramblings about known knowns, known unknowns and unknown unknowns. The Irish added another category: unknown knowns, things that were understood to be the case and yet remained unreal. At its most extreme this worked as a kind of collective psychosis, analogous to the idea of dissociation in psychiatry, where, in response to trauma, the mind distances itself from experiences that it does not wish to process.

This mechanism was at work in relation to corruption. Charles Haughey understood this with a clarity approaching genius. Instead of hiding the vast wealth for which an innocent explanation was impossible, he flaunted it, relying on the capacity of the public at large both to know that he must be corrupt and somehow to confine this knowledge to a dark corner of the brain where it remained inert and irrelevant. His success strengthened the workings of the unknown knowns – when his gargantuan appetite for other people's money was formally and undeniably revealed, it was necessary for the large swathe of the population that supported him to believe that it had not known about it all along. With this habit of mind so well ingrained it was possible to vote for a fraudster while believing that this was not an act of collusion but merely, for example, an expression of sympathy with a man who was good to his Mammy.

Gradually in this way, the Irish power of double-think became less charming and playful and more like George Orwell's definition of the word he invented in his novel *Nineteen Eighty-Four*: 'The power of holding two contradictory beliefs in one's mind simultaneously, and accepting both of them . . . To tell deliberate lies while genuinely believing in them, to forget any fact that has become inconvenient, and then, when it becomes necessary again, to draw it back from oblivion for just so long as it is needed, to deny the existence of objective reality and all the while to take account of the reality which one denies.'

Again, the consequences of this way of thinking were not abstract. The greatest unknown known of all was the fact that property prices were artificial and unsustainable. This was known both from history and from common sense. Economists and regulators knew it from studies and statistics. Ordinary punters knew through the operation of basic intelligence. It simply made no sense that a three-bedroomed semi in a Dublin suburb was 'worth' €1 million or that an apartment in Cork had the same value as a chateau on the Loire. Yet these realities were also unknown.

One contributor to the sense of displacement was undoubtedly the slow death of Catholic Ireland. The institutional Catholic Church had dominated both the public identity and the personal values of a majority of the population from the middle of the nineteenth century until the institution itself began to implode in the 1990s. The gradual rise of urban, secular and Anglo-American cultural norms on the one side and the revelation of horrific crimes of child abuse on the other broke that dominance. What the sociologist Tom Inglis called the 'moral monopoly' of the Church was ended.

For social conservatives, the loss of religious faith is an adequate explanation for the confusions of Irish life in the Celtic Tiger years and for the amorality that ran through them. But this explanation does not bear much scrutiny. In the first place, the Church was not a beacon of moral certitude – it was a deeply corrupt institution that tortured and enslaved children in its industrial schools and that placed the need to protect its own reputation by covering up child abuse ahead of the safety of vulnerable children. And secondly, the great nexus of amorality, Fianna Fáil, was arguably never more closely aligned with the Church than it was under Bertie Ahern. It was Ahern who passionately denounced as 'aggressive secularism' any attempt to debate the Church's continued control of the education and health systems. It was he who attempted to enshrine Catholic teaching on abortion in the constitution. Above all, it was he who used over €1 billion of public money to save the Church from the legal and financial consequences of its tolerance for child abuse when he agreed a deal to indemnify the religious orders against being sued. The institutional Church was not edged out by the governing culture of the Celtic Tiger – it was closely allied to it.

The real effect of the loss of Church authority was that there was no deeply rooted civic morality to take its place. The Irish had been taught for generations to identity morality with religion, and a very narrow kind of religion at that. Morality was about what happened in bedrooms, not in boardrooms. It was about the body, not the body politic. Masturbation was a much more serious sin than tax evasion. In a mindset where homosexuality was much worse than cooking the books, it was okay to be bent as long as you were straight. This nineteenth-century ethic was not pushed aside by the creation of a coherent and deeply rooted civic, democratic and social morality. It mostly collapsed under its own weight of hypocrisy. The familiar code of values, the language in which right and wrong could be discussed, lost its meaning before Irish society had fully learned to speak any other tongue.

One of the few areas of Irish life that had any continuing sense of integrity was artistic creativity. But here, too, there were no easy ways to get one's bearings. The last big economic and cultural shift, the opening up of the country to foreign investment in the late 1950s, had been played out with remarkable potency in the theatre, as a brilliant generation of playwrights (Brian Friel, Tom Murphy, Thomas Kilroy, John B. Keane) created vivid dramas of a society torn between past and future. This was possible because there was a single governing narrative – the conflict between tradition and modernity, between the local and the global, between the values of a rural, Catholic society and the aspirations of the young for personal freedom, emotional satisfaction and material abundance.

The problem with the world of the Celtic Tiger was that there wasn't a single big narrative that could be shaped into a clear conflict. The personal choices thrown up by social change were rather less heroic: agonising about whether to stay in a small village in Donegal or to emigrate to Philadelphia is rather more dramatic than wondering whether to buy a holiday home in Bulgaria or Florida. The sense of conflicted spaces (going into exile or staying at home) that shaped so much of the Irish artistic imagination in the twentieth century was not easy to generate for a generation that treated Ryanair like its bus service and did its Christmas shopping in New York. It is not for nothing that conflict (as opposed to bickering) virtually disappeared from Irish drama in the Celtic Tiger years and that monologue replaced dialogue as the preferred form for the younger writers.

A particular problem was that Ireland did not have a tradition of large-scale social realism. Irish history and society had been too angular, too discontinuous, for a realistic literature to thrive. Indeed, the glory of Irish writing had long been the distorting strangeness of the 'cracked looking glass' that did not so much reflect society as rearrange it into dreamily disconnected shapes. In the Celtic Tiger years, however, there were times when the country could have done with a kind of art that was forensically descriptive of contemporary Irish society, ordering its chaos into a recognisable whole. There were occasional triumphs of Irish realism on screen, like Lenny Abrahamson and Mark O'Halloran's superb conjuring of unofficial and invisible lives in *Adam and Paul*, *Prosperity* and *Garage*, or Eugene O'Brien and Declan Recks's micro-studies of Midlands anomie in *Pure Mule*. It was also true that the emergence of the Irish crime novel in such small masterpieces as Gene Kerrigan's *Little Criminals* and *Dark Times in the City* suggested that international genres like the thriller might be more useful in depicting a globalised culture than the more specifically Irish traditions proved to be. But no one in any form could manage the kind of realist epic that would give a multi-layered and shifting society a sense of where it was and how it got there.

It may have been, in fact, that the disruptions of time and space in boomtime Ireland were simply too complex to be dealt with in the same work. On the whole, Irish literature was far better at dealing with time than with space. It had relatively easy access to a framework – the extended family – in which time unfolds naturally. The great familial myths of Sebastian Barry or Marina Carr, or the more intense and intimate worlds of, say, Anne Enright's *The Gathering*, were very powerful correctives to the sense of a continuous, timeless present tense that dominated the boom years. They reminded people that the past doesn't just go away.

On the other hand, the rarer engagements with the fractured sense of space (Tom Murphy's *The House*, say, or Colm

Tóibín's novel *Brooklyn*) dealt with the idea of living in two places at the same time, but did so by projecting themselves backwards to an era long before the Celtic Tiger was even imaginable. On the whole, it was easier to deal with that unruly beast either by confining it within the cage of familial intimacies or by seeking the possibility of narrative order in older, more distant settings.

There was also the paradox that the most thoroughly globalised brand of Irish culture in the boom years was also the most conservative. Aspects of Irish culture were commodified as never before in boybands, popular women's fiction and Irish dancing shows. At least the first two of those, however, tended to be peculiarly archaic. The Boyzones and Westlifes were little more than the Irish showbands of the 1960s, scrubbed up, slicked down and without the cumbersome need to play instruments or be particularly good at music. The popular fiction writers who sold vast numbers of books in shiny covers around the world were of very mixed quality, but in broad terms their work derived (at worst) from jazzed-up Mills and Boon and (at best) from the Irish short-story tradition of the 1930s. In both cases, the trick was to package and market aspects of pre-Celtic Tiger Irish culture as globalised commodities, not to actually respond in any real way to contemporary Ireland.

One of the real markers of this was sex. It is a lavish understatement to say that Irish sexual mores changed in the 1990s. Yet, while the end of the Franco era in Spain, which produced a surge of sexual energy in a previously repressed Catholic country, gave the world Pedro Almódovar and Penélope Cruz, the breaking of Ireland's sexual Berlin wall gave the world Boyzone. What the boybands and much of the chicklit shared was a strangely antiseptic, coy sexuality.

They were, after all, sometimes overlapping worlds: in Cecelia Ahern's *P.S. I Love You*, the heroine dreams of listening to 'the soothing sounds of her favourite Westlife CD'. The same heroine has a 'neat little chest' instead of breasts, and on being given a present by a friend giggles, 'It's a battery operated . . . oh my God! Ciara! You naughty girl!'

The dance shows, however, did, in an odd way, respond to the changing nature of the Celtic Tiger – they got infinitely worse. *Riverdance*, which created the genre and became the most commercially successful Irish cultural export of all time, was actually a highly sophisticated piece of work. It created and enacted a myth that really did capture something about the way Irish people hoped to see themselves in the 1990s. It took a traditional and rather despised form – Irish dancing – and injected it with the steroids of sex, speed, Irish-American optimism and fake tan. But it was a genuine synthesis of traditional forms and music (composed and performed by people who really understood and valued it) on the one hand and Broadway pizzazz on the other.

And its narrative was actually the nearest thing the first phase of the Celtic Tiger created to a myth of itself. It played out a story of globalisation (Irish dancing evolving in the mists of time, being taken to America by emigrants, fusing with other cultures, and then, by implication, returning on the winged feet of Michael Flatley and Jean Butler) that was also a comforting narrative of cyclical continuity. What was coming to Ireland now was simply what had left it before. Life in a multicultural society wasn't a threat to tradition, but an enhancement of it. Along with the spectacle and the show-biz, *Riverdance* was a statement about how it was possible to be Irish in the twenty-first century.

If *Riverdance* was the great mythic spectacle of the first

phase of the Irish boom, before it became a bubble, the characteristic spectacle of the second part, appropriately enough, was Michael Flatley's 2005 show *The Celtic Tiger*. In its precisely calibrated mixture of stupidity and lavishness, it was the perfect show for a society that had more money than sense.

The Celtic Tiger broadly replayed the narrative of *Riverdance*, from the Celtic mists of time to American emigration to cultural fusion to triumphant transatlantic return. But this time it was not a broad metaphor for the globalisation of Irish culture, but quite specifically the unfolding in dance, song and spectacle of the Celtic Tiger itself. The tiger was now the prime emblem of Ireland – two huge, Disneyfied tiger faces flanked the screens and one of the climactic dances featured slinky women in tiger-striped costumes crawling, pawing and rubbing themselves in ecstasy (house prices must have been up again) as if they were escapees from a porn remake of *Cats*.

The extravagant ludicrousness of *The Celtic Tiger* did not make it any less authentic an expression of its subject matter. Indeed it probably made it more so. One of the fascinations of the show was its high kitsch presentation of Irish history as a pure pastiche in which whole eras melt into each other. Thus, it began with Flatley dressed presumably as a Celtic warrior but actually as a cross between a particularly louche Roman general (Caligula playing at soldiers perhaps) and Elvis Presley in Las Vegas. All Irish history is sweet – up to a point. Devout monks dervish-dance with lurid temptresses, with nary a word about the corruptions of the flesh. Horny-headed Vikings dance chastely with Irish maidens. An Irish Garden of Eden blossoms.

But then the chorus line of Brits invades, identifiable by

their red coats and powdered wigs, goose-stepping and robotic, like clockwork Nazis. They burn a thatched cottage. (The Irish maidens barely escape the fire, but, distressingly, the bottom three-quarters of their skirts have been consumed by the flames.) There is much writhing around to indicate the Famine. Father Michael Flatley enters in a nineteenth-century soutane intoning the Lord's Prayer. The Brits surround him and shoot him dead with their fingers. A man sings 'The Four Green Fields' (a traditional nineteenth-century ballad written in the late 1960s). A boy playing, of all things, soccer is blown up by a British tank (presumably one of the little known nineteenth-century prototypes exclusively used for oppressing the Irish). Then Michael Flatley leads the 1916 Rising. It is not surprising that he wins, since the Brits are still in their redcoats and powdered wigs and are still using their fingers for guns. Everybody sings 'A Nation Once Again'. Ireland is free and triumphant.

But there's not much to do in Ireland now that it's free, so everyone goes to New York. They dance with homeboys and Spaniards and Michael dances dressed as a gangster with nifty spats and a Tommy gun, so he's clearly doing well. But what of Ireland back home? It's struggling to become modern: here's Kathleen ni Houlihan as an Aer Lingus stewardess in a green uniform, dancing a jig in high heels – modernity and tradition. Then Michael and his crew of sun-glassed beefcake boys in Pan Am uniforms fly her over New York. She sees Ireland's destiny. She does a striptease act, peeling off her green Irish uniform to reveal underneath a bra and panties imprinted with the Stars and Stripes. Ireland was really America all along and now the Celtic Tiger has allowed itself to reveal its true identity. All that suffering – the Famine, the evictions, the murder of Saint Michael Flatley by the redcoat Brit bastards – has been repaid at last. Flatley leads the chorus line in a big, rapturous tap-along to 'Yankee Doodle Dandy'. The triumph has come: we are real live cousins of our Uncle Sam.

Risible as all of this is, it is the best that Irish culture could do in constructing a mythic version of the meaning of the Celtic Tiger in its manic, delusional phase. It was crass and bloated, vulgar and ridiculous, but it came to a conclusion that made some kind of sense: Ireland is not Ireland any more but someplace else. And it came up with a name for that place: America.

There were other names too, of course: Bermuda, Liechtenstein, Dubai. And they were all attempts to escape from a reality that would ultimately assert itself, the real society behind the dreamy facades.

9

Fair Play to You, Willie

'The world watched in astonishment. That is no exaggeration.'
– Seán FitzPatrick, chairman of Anglo Irish Bank

In late November 2008, there was a business lunch in the pavilion at Leopardstown racecourse. The star turns were the former Taoiseach Bertie Ahern and his old pal Seánie, more formally known as Seán FitzPatrick, chairman of Ireland's third largest bank, Anglo Irish. Less than two months previously, Fitzpatrick's bank had precipitated a crisis that led to a state guarantee of all deposits in Irish banks. Yet both Bertie and Seánie were on jovial form. Both referred to the coming end of the recession, which they both called 'the other side of the hill'. Bertie quipped, in relation to the venue, that 'If you can't make money any other way, you can try it on a horse.' Anyway, he added to cheer up his listeners, 'I think Seánie has a bit left.'

Less than a month later, on 18 December 2008, Seánie resigned as chairman of Anglo Irish. It had emerged that FitzPatrick had €84 million in loans from his own bank. The lending was approved by the bank's credit committee and known to its internal auditor. Anglo Irish had, however, been cooking its books to hide these liabilities from shareholders and potential investors. Each year, as the deadline for the annual accounts approached, FitzPatrick borrowed whatever amount he owed to Anglo from a building society, Irish Nationwide. The auditors would examine the books and see no holes. Within a few days, FitzPatrick repaid the money to Nationwide. The sums involved were huge: at one stage in 2007, FitzPatrick's loans amounted to €129 million and in June 2009 the figure stood at €106 million. The purpose of the operation was entirely straightforward – to hide the fact that Seánie was taking large chunks of the bank's cash for a private gambling spree on Irish and international property, the financing of films and the purchase of shares in Anglo Irish itself. Fitzpatrick had been doing this end-of-year financial shuffle for eight years, to the tune of €228 million in total.

Even more bizarre than this juggling act at a supposedly reputable bank, however, was the fact that the Financial Regulator knew about it. Anglo Irish didn't tell the regulator, and its auditors Ernst and Young never managed to spot the strange pattern of money coming in from Irish Nationwide and flowing out again, always between 26 and 30 September of each year. But Irish Nationwide's auditors, KPMG, had warned its directors of the 'reputational risk' from the loans. The building society, in turn, had covered its own behind by informing the Regulator. As Irish Nationwide's chairman Danny Kitchen explained in a formal statement in May 2009, 'The Society, in line with its normal reporting procedures, informed the Regulator of this loan amongst others and at no time was any adverse comment received.'

More outlandish still was the reaction, in December 2008, of the Financial Regulator, the government and the Minister for Finance Brian Lenihan to the revelations. Firstly, the Regulator, Pat Neary, confirmed that his office 'became aware, following an inspection earlier this year, of matters surrounding loans from Anglo Irish Bank to Seán FitzPatrick'. It had merely 'advised Anglo Irish Bank to ensure that these loans are reported in the annual accounts for 2008' – please stop cooking the books. But this was not a matter of any great consequence since 'it does not appear that anything illegal took place in relation to these loans'. The highest pitch of indignation the Financial Regulator could manage was to mutter that 'the practices surrounding these loans were not appropriate'.

It was not hard to understand this urge to slap Seánie about the head with a feather. The Financial Regulator, under Neary, had known about FitzPatrick's dodgy back-to-back loans for years from Irish Nationwide's reports, had actually spotted them in the Anglo Irish accounts early in 2008 and had done next to nothing. However personally uncomfortable individual supervisors may have been, the Financial Regulator was institutionally bound to underplay the affair. If FitzPatrick's book-cookery had been illegal, then the Financial Regulator had failed to stop a crime. It followed, therefore, that nothing illegal can have occurred.

But this standard exercise in corporate arse-covering also became official government policy. Just as Ireland's international reputation was disappearing over the horizon, the crew of the ship sent a signal to shore – it's perfectly legal to doctor your annual accounts in Ireland.

Brian Lenihan issued a statement on behalf of the government. It 'expressed his disappointment at the circumstances surrounding the resignation of Mr Seán FitzPatrick as chairman' of Anglo Irish.

Disappointment had always been the emotion of choice for Fianna Fáil and other members of the Irish establishment confronted with scams, swindles and con-jobs by respectable bankers. Charlie McCreevy, as Minister for Finance in 2000, commented on the revelation of the DIRT conspiracy: 'I must again say that the standards the public are entitled to expect were not adhered to in many financial institutions, and that was very disappointing.' Bertie Ahern, in the same year, was 'gravely disappointed' that a member of his party, Denis Foley, was part of the Ansbacher scam. The Moriarty report into the way his mentor Charles Haughey trousered the equivalent of €45 million was also, funnily enough, a cause of 'grave disappointment'.

Being disappointed was Fianna Fáil's default mode when faced with crookery. Instead of reflecting on the ways in which they might have colluded with the behaviour in question, it allowed them to present themselves as victims whose feelings had been quite terribly hurt.

Lenihan's insipid statement was a signal that the government was adopting as its own position both FitzPatrick's claim in his resignation statement that his behaviour has been merely 'inappropriate from a transparency point of view' and the Regulator's self-serving insistence that nothing illegal had been done. These two positions were in fact conflated by the Tánaiste (deputy prime minister) Mary Coughlan later the same day when she said of Lenihan: 'As he said, he is disappointed about the actions, although not illegal.' It was now official government policy, broadcast to the world, that Seán FitzPatrick had broken no laws when he shifted tens of millions of euro off the books and into his own investment schemes eight years in a row.

Lenihan's and Coughlan's statements were among the stupidest ever made by an Irish government – a significant achievement in itself. There were just two possible conclusions that any rational international observer could have drawn. One was that cooking the books is actually illegal in Ireland, but that the authorities were rushing to protect a well-got banker with strong connections to the ruling party. The other was that naked deception is perfectly legal in Ireland and that you can't trust the accounts of any Irish-regulated company. The *Independent* newspaper of London reported that 'Analysts were also stunned that the practice was not illegal in Ireland.' The *Financial Times* called Ireland a banana republic. The description in 2005 by the *New York Times* of Dublin as 'the Wild West of European finance' was widely revived. The thin shred of credibility that covered the Irish banking system's global reputation was torn asunder.

And all of this happened because Fianna Fáil simply could not bring itself to acknowledge the emerging truth that, institutionally, Anglo Irish was as bent as a Brazilian free kick. The party went even deeper into denial when Lenihan appeared on RTE radio and tried to undo the damage. He firstly denied that he had used the word 'disappointing' about FitzPatrick's resignation: 'No, I never said I was disappointed.' He had in fact, he claimed, used the word only in relation to the failure of the Financial Regulator to inform his department of the loans. This was flatly untrue on both counts. Even more strangely, having tried to rewrite his own reaction to the scandal, Lenihan then went on to rewrite Fitz-Patrick's contemptible statement about 'inappropriate' behaviour: 'I believe it was, as he himself acknowledged in his statement, wrong, unethical behaviour.' FitzPatrick's statement did not contain the words 'wrong' or 'unethical' or any synonyms of those words. They would have stood out as startlingly in his self-regarding announcement as a call for a worker's revolution. Lenihan was convincing himself, as much as his listeners, that concepts of right and wrong truly applied in the Irish financial system. What we had in effect was the surreal situation of the Minister for Finance spinning for a banker who was involved in large-scale systematic deception.

Where did this need for denial come from? In part, it was rooted in the general cosiness of the relationship between government politicians, regulators and bankers. There was a broad ideological consensus that the free market knows best and that it was wise to let the money-makers take care of business. In spite of the often farcically lax state of regulation, a self-pitying belief that they were under siege from voracious, busybody bureaucrats was a standard item of gossip around the exclusive golf courses on which the insiders mingled.

Seán FitzPatrick himself was the loudest champion of this world view. In one swaggering speech in 2005, at the *Irish Times* Property Awards, Seánie paid tribute to people like himself who had created the boom: 'we had ideas and we had balls . . . as we worked the scene and maximised the moment, the world watched in astonishment. That is no exaggeration.' But there were clouds on the previously clear horizon. Where the boom had been enabled by 'a positive environment where risk-taking was applauded and success rewarded', there were now two forces that threatened everything. One was 'the quite hostile approach towards business by elements in the media'. He moaned that 'issues of compliance or general corporate conduct get coverage that is disproportionate to their importance, or the frequency with which they would arise'. The state broadcaster RTE, he complained, had given airtime to people who were critical of the running of the economy. This commentary could 'support a political agenda that is far removed from any of our long-established political parties'. 'This whole area', he warned darkly, 'needs attention.'

The other dragon that Seánie wished to slay, though, was regulation. 'Moves towards greater control and regulation could squeeze the life out of an economy that has thrived on intuition, imagination and a spirit of adventure.' There were, he informed his horrified listeners, 'those who appear to want to establish Ireland as the perfect model in corporate policing and regulation'. What, he demanded in one of the great rhetorical questions of the Celtic Tiger era, 'has been done here over the past decade that demands such a reaction?'

Since corporate Ireland was so patently pure and honest, demands for regulation could only come from paranoid maniacs: in a speech in June 2007 FitzPatrick actually called regulation 'corporate McCarthyism [that] shouldn't be tolerated'. The truth, of course, was that if the Irish financial regulator was the House Un-American Activities Committee, the US would would have been overrun by Communist infiltrators.

But if FitzPatrick epitomised the self-image of much of the Celtic Tiger elite – men with big balls whom the world watched in astonishment while petty media folk whinged about corporate conduct – he also epitomised its arrogant disregard for either basic ethics or sustainable business practices.

In Fianna Fáil and its hinterland, FitzPatrick inspired awe. Having joined Anglo's precursor in 1974, when he was twenty-six and it was a tiny niche bank, he turned it into the chariot on which Ireland's property developers would ride to the stars. In 1985, Anglo had profits of IR£286,000. In 2007, the figure was €1.2 billion.

The graph of Fitzpatrick's success matched and indeed surpassed the rising euphoria of the boom years. In 2001, Anglo had assets of €15.8 billion. By 2008, the assets were within touching distance of €100 billion. It had €44 billion in loans in the Republic of Ireland, €21 billion in the UK and €9.5 billion in the US. Anglo was a rocket blazing across the skies of Bertie Ahern's Ireland, illuminating the money-strewn landscape beneath.

FitzPatrick mattered to Fianna Fáil as an exemplar of success, but he also had a more practical importance. Fitz-Patrick's bank funded the property developers who helped to fund Fianna Fáil. Big players and party supporters like Bernard McNamara (a former party councillor), Mick Bailey, Seán Dunne, Seán Mulryan, Gerry Gannon, Johnny Ronan and Seamus Ross were on Anglo's books. Two of these men had made large payments to corrupt politicians. Bailey gave Ray Burke £30,000 or £40,000 in 1989, on foot of a promise to 'procure' re-zoning for a development in North Dublin – the Flood tribunal found this to be a corrupt payment. Ross gave the notorious Fianna Fáil fixer Liam Lawlor £40,000 in two tranches in 1996 to have the postal address of a new housing estate he had built changed from Clondalkin to the more upmarket Lucan – a move he believed would make the houses worth an extra £5,000 each.

None of the other Anglo Irish clients made such payments to crooked politicians. They were, however, generous contributors of legitimate political donations to Fianna Fáil. And they often moved within the same social circles as senior politicians. Seán Mulryan's annual Christmas parties at his Kildare stud farm, Ardenode, were just one of the social occasions when FitzPatrick and his developer clients would have mingled intimately with Charlie McCreevy and Brian Cowen. The personal connections within these circles were strong: Ross was close to Brian Lenihan and his brother (and junior minister) Conor, Mulryan to McCreevy. At the 2009 Cheltenham racing festival, for example, McCreevy and his wife shared a box (just below the royal box) with Mulryan and Mick Bailey. Seán Dunne built McCreevy's substantial home in County Kildare. Dunne's personal assistant, Anto Kelly, is a former election agent for the ex-minister and current Ceann Comhairle (chairman of the Dáil), John O'Donoghue.

Fitzpatrick's Anglo Irish was the quintessential developers' bank. Business banking and personal banking each accounted for just 5 per cent of its loan book. Two-thirds of its lending was for 'investment' purposes, but these investments were almost all in property: hotels, offices, shopping centres, residential developments. A further 15 per cent was in land. And most of the rest was in development. By 2008, a quarter of Anglo's loans, amounting to €17.7 billion, were to developers. Over €6.5 billion of this was lent for the purest form of speculation – the purchase of land which had no full planning permission for projects.

And the bulk of the €17.7 billion was lent to a tiny circle of high rollers. Anglo had fifteen clients, almost certainly developers, each of whom had at least €500 million in loans. The top twenty clients owed it a total of €11.4 billion. In the UK and US markets (often in relation to the same Irish developers), the top twenty customers accounted for 46 per cent and 32 per cent of the development loan book respectively.

Not only was Anglo far too exposed to the speculative property game, but even within that narrow field it was massively dependent on a very small number of risk-taking individuals. But FitzPatrick and his acolytes considered this a virtue. The bank's relationship with its inner circle of clients was not just business, it was personal. As Anglo explained to Price Waterhouse Coopers in November 2008, 'this strategy of developing deep relationships with what it deems to be the strongest operators is deliberate . . . Anglo considers itself able to attain a thorough understanding of its clients' business, finances and relevant risks, which are continually reassessed in face to face client meetings often held weekly.' A shared culture of macho risk-taking and go-getting, and shared hobbies like horse-racing, golf and Fianna Fáil, undoubtedly helped these 'deep relationships' to flourish. It may be an exaggeration to call Anglo Irish a private bank for Fianna Fáil's more flamboyant friends, but only a small one.

The centrality of Anglo Irish to the nexus of connections between Fianna Fáil and the developers was recognised in appointments to key state boards. The Dublin Airport Authority was chaired by Anglo director Gary McGann. His colleague Anne Heraty was appointed to the boards of Bord na Mona and Forfas. But the plum jobs were reserved for FitzPatrick himself He was on the board of the state-owned airline Aer Lingus. Alongside yet another Anglo Irish director, Lar Bradshaw, he was also on the board of the Dublin Docklands Development Authority, giving him a direct influence on the state's own largest property development project. Effectively, Fitzpatrick was able to fuse the interests of the DDDA with those of Anglo Irish. In 2006, the DDDA was part of a consortium led by the developer Bernard McNamara that paid a phenomenal €412 million for the 24-acre Irish Glass Bottle site in Poolbeg on the docklands. Fitz-Patrick at Anglo Irish put up €288 million in loans for the project. (Davy Stockbrokers, in 2009, advised its clients who had put money into the deal to write off 60 per cent of their investment.)

For all this eminent respectability, however, Anglo Irish was a house of cards with too many knaves in the deck.

Extraordinary as it was, the annual cooking of the books to conceal FitzPatrick's vast loans from his own bank was a mere *amuse-bouche*. The main courses of chicanery and fiddling would be served as the bank's inevitable collapse approached.

Anglo Irish's over-exposure to both developers and investments in property was inherently unsustainable. Without a perpetually rising property market in which its key clients could service ever more extravagant borrowings to fund ever more outlandish projects, Anglo Irish's own phenomenal growth could not continue. As the air began to leak out of the property balloon, Anglo Irish was bound to lose altitude at the velocity of a falling stone.

On 6 March 2008, almost half a billion euro was knocked off Anglo's share value in a single day after it announced that it was taking a write-down on risky assets and adopting a more conservative approach to future lending. The very fact that the announcement that a bank intends to be careful in its lending caused a run on its shares is eloquent testimony to the fantastical nature of Anglo Irish itself. Punters realised that a cautious Anglo is like a vegetarian lion or a gentle boxer – essentially redundant. From what had been a slow descent from a high of €17.85 in June 2007, the bank's shares tumbled steadily towards worthlessness. By October 2008 they would be worth €1.13, and by Christmas they had shrivelled to a barely visible €0.15.

It was in the attempt to halt or at least conceal this decline, however, that Anglo really took to snorkelling in the cesspit. In its rage against the dying of FitzPatrick's dreams of astonishing the world, his bank managed to make a fine international spectacle of itself. His notions of 'working the scene and maximising the moment' fulfilled themselves in two breathtaking schemes to create the illusion that Anglo was not a beaten docket but still a winning lottery ticket.

The first of these schemes had its roots, appropriately enough, in Fianna Fáil's extreme attentiveness to the demands of the financial industry. In 2006, in one those behind-the-scenes manoeuvres that attract no attention beyond a tiny circle of insiders, the finance lobby managed to head off a simple proposal by the Revenue Commissioners. It related to devices of whose existence 99.9 per cent of the population was blissfully ignorant: contracts for difference (CFDs). A CFD is a form of derivative instrument that allows an investor to bet on the likely performance of a particular stock, without actually owning the shares. Because the investors didn't buy the shares, they didn't pay stamp duty to the Revenue. To counteract this, the Revenue wanted to charge stamp duty on the shares that were actually bought to cover the CFDs. It believed that it was entitled to do this under existing law, and made an announcement to this effect.

As well as closing a tax loophole, this measure would have had the considerable advantage of discouraging the use of CFDs. A major attraction of this form of gambling was precisely that it avoided tax. Another key incentive was that holders of CFDs did not have to declare their interest in the company whose shares they were betting on. And nowhere was this measure more necessary than in Ireland: nearly a third of the value of trades on the Irish Stock Exchange was accounted for by CFDs. From the point of view of both fairer taxation and the discouragement of casino capitalism, the Revenue's modest proposal was obviously in the public interest.

The then Minister for Finance, Brian Cowen, was lobbied, however, by the Irish Stock Exchange, the London Investment Banking Association, Davy Stockbrokers and Price Waterhouse Coopers. The money men got exactly what they wanted. Cowen announced that he would 'have the matter reviewed in advance of the next Budget'. Predictably that budget slapped down the Revenue. It created a new category of tax shelter, Intermediary Relief, specifically tailored to ensure that shares bought by brokers to cover CFDs would not be subject to stamp duty. The casino would remain open for business, and the punters could retain their privacy.

Stepping up to the table with uncharacteristic brio was a man who had been thought of as Ireland's most astute entrepreneur, Seán Quinn. Quinn, whose building supplies, insurance and manufacturing businesses had made him Ireland's richest man, unaccountably decided to invest much of his fortune in Anglo Irish. At the highest point of stock market euphoria over the bank's stellar profits, he began to take out CFDs on its shares. He gambled somewhere between €2 billion and €3 billion on Anglo Irish. In almost any other developed country, such a huge punt on the stock market would at least be an open transaction. In Ireland, because of Cowen's capitulation to the financial lobby, Quinn's enormous wager entered the Celtic informational twilight of things that are known but not known.

There was no public record of the fact that Quinn, through his CFDs, effectively owned 25 per cent of Anglo Irish. But Anglo's own board knew, and because it was unsure what Quinn was up to, it told the Financial Regulator. By March 2008, the Regulator had passed the word on to the Minister for Finance, Brian Cowen. Rumours abounded and contributed to the sharp fall in Anglo's share price. But no one 'knew' anything and no one had to do anything.

Eventually, it was Quinn himself who broke cover. With

the shares losing value by the day, he decided to both regularise and reduce his 25 per cent holding in the bank. He would sell 10 per cent and convert the other 15 per cent from CFDs into ordinary shares. From this decision flowed two scandalous transactions.

Firstly, to help pay for his 15 per cent stake, Quinn dipped into the reserves of Quinn Insurance, of which he was also chief executive, taking a loan of €288 million. This was so egregious a breach of the financial laws that even the Financial Regulator had to act: Quinn's company was fined €3.2 million with an additional personal penalty of €200,000. Secondly, Anglo Irish, concerned that the sudden sale of the other 10 per cent would drive its shares even further into the ground, concocted an extravagant scam to keep them off the market and thus to artificially support the share price.

The scheme was the apotheosis of the culture of 'deep relationships' that Anglo Irish had exemplified. It was also the culmination of the love of 'back-to-back' transactions that had been woven into that culture since the Ansbacher Cayman days. Under pressure, the Anglo Irish bosses went for a spin on a good old-fashioned carousel. They assembled a group of trusted pals and lent them €451 million so that they, in turn, could buy Quinn's remaining 10 per cent stake in Anglo Irish. The terms of these loans were appropriately soft: 25 per cent of the money was secured against the borrowers' personal assets, the rest against the shares themselves. In this hall of mirrors the unstable Anglo Irish shares were both the object of the loans and the supposed guarantee that they would be repaid. (Mostly, they have not been: in May 2009, Anglo – now in effect the Irish taxpayer – wrote off €308 million on the deal.)

The names of six of the ten members of this so-called 'gold-

en circle' of investors are known. One, Jerry Conlon, specialised in building and developing private hospitals and has
no recorded Fianna Fáil connections. Four of the others are
typical of the nexus of pro-Fianna Fáil developers whose
projects were funded by Anglo Irish. Paddy McKillen, a
developer, was appointed to the Construction Industry Development Board by Fianna Fáil minister Padraig Flynn in 1989
and made at least one donation to the Fianna Fáil politician
Tom Kitt. Joe O'Reilly, whose €575 million purchase of a
shopping centre in north Dublin in 2006 was described by the
Irish Times as 'the largest and most significant property
investment ever completed in Ireland', was a friend and
financial supporter of the Fianna Fáil TD Seán Ardagh. In
2000, he was a member of the 'Friends of Seán Ardagh Committee' that raised IR£14,000 for the TD's campaigns. Seamus Ross, as we have seen, gave £40,000 to Liam Lawlor.
Gerry Gannon, who amassed a huge land bank around
Dublin, is close to the Bailey brothers, and donated money to
the then Fianna Fáil TD Ivor Callely in 2006. He was one of
the small group of attendees at a private fundraising dinner
given in Dublin in November 2007 by Brian Cowen. The
sixth known member of the circle, the Dublin estate agent
Brian O'Farrell, was one of a group of thirteen businessmen
who collectively paid €65,000 for a private meeting with
Brian Cowen in March 2008. He subsequently told the *Mail
on Sunday* that 'I am not in Fianna Fáil' and that the meeting,
in the Shelbourne Hotel, was 'just like a normal chat'.

Lending these people €450 million to buy its shares and
make it look to other investors as if Anglo Irish was weather-
ing the storm might seem like the height of the bank's effrontery. But there were further heights to be scaled and Anglo
Irish was willing to climb every mountain.

From March 2008, when Anglo Irish's share price began its rapid descent, the bank was colluding with another major financial institution, Irish Life and Permanent (ILP), to make Anglo's deposit base look healthier than it really was. Again, the mechanism of choice was to place a chunk of money on a merry-go-round and give it a good spin. At the end of that month, Anglo Irish put €1 billion into an ILP subsidiary and ILP in turn deposited €750 million in Anglo Irish.

This was merely a prelude to a much larger carousel of cash in September, as Anglo's end-of-year deadline for reporting its accounts approached. In the last week of September, Anglo's situation was becoming desperate as €5.4 billion in corporate and retail deposits was withdrawn by anxious customers. It went back to ILP for a repeat of the March exercise on a vastly larger scale. In five separate deposits between 26 and 29 September, ILP put €3.45 billion into Anglo Irish, receiving the same sum in cash from the bank. On 30 September, the last day of Anglo's financial year, the same trick was repeated, this time to the tune of €4 billion. (This €7.45 billion was nearly six times the entire market value of ILP itself.) Crucially, these vast sums were listed, not as inter-bank deposits, but as 'customer deposits'. The aim, purely and simply, was to deceive anyone looking at the accounts into thinking that Anglo was still a viable bank into which sane people were depositing huge amounts of cash. In particular, the loan-to-deposit ratio, by which investors judge the soundness of a bank, was distorted. It was actually around 160 per cent. The scam made it look like a much healthier 140 per cent.

The brazen mendacity of Anglo Irish – concealing the huge loans to FitzPatrick and other directors, rigging the sale of its own shares and doctoring its accounts to the tune of €7.45

billion – could be seen as merely the most lurid chapter in the sordid saga of Irish banking's dodgy deals. Except that, tragically, it was also the trigger for probably the most disastrous decision ever made by an Irish government.

On the night of 29 September 2008, a small delegation of senior Irish bankers arrived at Government Buildings in Dublin to meet Cowen, Lenihan, the attorney general Paul Gallagher, the Financial Regulator Pat Neary and the governor of the Central Bank, John Hurley. Earlier that day, bank shares had taken a huge hit on the Irish stock exchange, with Allied Irish Bank falling by 15 per cent. The context was obvious enough – the international banking crisis, the known over-exposure of all the Irish banks to inflated property values and, in particular, the knowledge that Anglo Irish was in deep trouble. It was Anglo Irish shares that took the biggest fall, dropping by 46 per cent. If the banking sector as a whole was a cause for alarm, it was Anglo Irish that was the cause for panic.

The banking delegation came from the two largest institutions: Brian Goggin and Richard Burrows of Bank of Ireland, Eugene Sheehy and Dermot Gleeson of AIB. Afterwards, the crisis meeting would be presented as an emergency summit aimed at saving those banks. But it was not that, or at least not directly. There was no immediate threat that BOI or AIB were about to go under. If they were the primary concern, the obvious course was to consult quickly with the European Central Bank and the other governments in the eurozone and to see what kind of co-ordinated intervention they were planning for what was, after all, a much broader crisis.

The immediate issue, in reality, was Anglo Irish. While very little has been revealed about what really took place that night, one intriguing detail has slipped out. In January 2009, in angrily denying a claim in the *Irish Times* that his officials had recommended not attempting to save Anglo Irish, Brian Lenihan told the Dáil that in fact: 'The only legislation before the Taoiseach and I on that evening [29 September] was a Bill which, in all material terms, is the same as the Bill before the House today.' The Bill before the Dáil as he said this was one to nationalise Anglo Irish Bank.

What happened, therefore, is that the Department of Finance officials went into the emergency meeting with a draft bill for the nationalisation of Anglo Irish. This in itself was hugely problematic, but it made some sense. Nationalising Anglo Irish would buy some breathing space in which the government could work with the rest of the EU on a co-ordinated response to the broader crisis. Yet, for some reason – whether an ideological hang-up about nationalisation or a residual loyalty to Seán FitzPatrick or a mixture of both – Cowen and Lenihan decided not to take this course.

The outcome of the late-night session was a decision to leap straight into the expanding pool of darkness that was the Irish banking system. Seánie and his acolytes would be left in charge at Anglo Irish and the fiction that it was a viable bank would be maintained. Instead, all six major Irish financial institutions, including Anglo Irish, would have their 'deposits, loans and obligations' guaranteed 100 per cent by the Irish taxpayer. The government had effectively no idea what those obligations were or how many of the loans were likely to be repaid.

This decision stunned and enraged Ireland's European partners and began a process by which the state would move, step by step, into underwriting all the excesses of the banks and developers over the Celtic Tiger years. At least two generations of Irish people would be made to pay for the blind folly and greed of a closed elite. But the decision to guarantee all of Anglo's obligations was particularly breathtaking. Banks like BOI and AIB were clearly a crucial part of the real Irish economy. Anglo was a bubble bank, a chimerical creation of the years of swagger and self-delusion. Lenihan would later claim, when Anglo Irish had to be nationalised anyway, that it was 'of systemic importance to Ireland'. The only Ireland in which it was of systemic importance was the one you could fly over in a Lear jet or a helicopter.

The irony is that by opting to sustain the illusion that Anglo could go on as a private bank under FitzPatrick, the government made it inevitable that it would have to be nationalised anyway. As scandal after scandal was revealed, the bank became more toxic than a chemical weapons dump. Having effectively taken over responsibility for that dump, the government ended up owning it. It did so in the worst possible circumstances, making the Irish people the proud possessors of an institution that had become notorious even in a world where sleazy bankers were falling like rain.

A crucial question here is how much the government knew about the extent to which Anglo was cooking its books. The amazing shenanigans that were going on in the bank on the days before and after the crisis meeting of 29 September would surely suggest to any sane government that Anglo should be treated like radioactive waste, to be isolated and contained, not coddled and embraced.

The Financial Regulator certainly had a good idea of what was going on. Daily liquidity reports provided to his office by Anglo in late September and early October would have revealed that it was receiving multi-billion euro deposits. On 24 September, five days before the government decided on its guarantee, Pat Neary held a meeting with Anglo's finance director Willie McAteer and CEO David Drumm. According to the *Sunday Tribune*'s account of a confidential Anglo Irish audit report, McAteer told Neary that 'the bank would be "managing the balance sheet at year end"', meaning that Anglo would be cooking its books to make the situation at the end of its financial year (30 September) look healthy. The report records Neary as replying, 'Fair play to you, Willie.'

The Financial Regulator's office later claimed that what it understood to be under discussion at that meeting were legitimate inter-bank deposits, not phoney customer deposits. But a recording of a phone call on 1 October between Anglo and the Regulator's office seems to indicate that the bank was quite open about what it was doing. Asked about the €8 billion in deposits that had mysteriously appeared in the previous few days, the bank official said, 'It's trying to manipulate our balance sheet for our financial year-end last night . . . We boosted our customer funding number so when our snapshot is produced at the beginning of December it will look as good as possible.'

It is hard to believe that, right at the moment when the state was taking on Anglo's obligations, no one told the government that the institution was systematically misleading its shareholders and investors. Brian Lenihan later told the Dáil that even though Price Waterhouse Coopers informed his officials of the back-to-back deposits in October, he did not know about them until the bank was nationalised in January 2009. Incredible as it seems, the reality that the state was making its citizens responsible for an institution whose books were the most inventive work of Irish fiction since *Ulysses* was not grasped by the government.

There was perhaps a certain kind of poetic justice in all of this. A system that had spent decades not wanting to know plunged itself into decades of likely misery because of what it didn't know. A culture of denial in which regulators learned not to raise awkward subjects and civil servants avoided subjects their political masters might not want to discuss reached its ironic conclusion. When sharp-eyed scrutiny had become a matter of national survival, the long-ingrained habit of looking the other way could not be shaken.

The Second Republic

'When you don't believe something, you can't achieve it.
You have to imagine, and make that imagination achievable.'
– Muhammad Yunus

It was fun while it lasted. For about six years, from the mid-1990s until late 2001, Ireland felt free – at last. Free from the pain and bitterness of forced emigration. Free from the sense of inferiority that comes with a long history of failure (and the exaggerated, defensive national self-regard that always accompanies and shadows that emotion). Free from the hopeless feeling of being locked into an insoluble ethnic and sectarian conflict. Free from the authoritarian religiosity that compensated for the absence of civic morality. Free from the need to celebrate picturesque poverty as a way of making a virtue of grim necessity.

In those years, Ireland was raw and sometimes vulgar. It was poorly led and hampered by a lack of long-term vision and genuine public ambition. It was chaotic, sometimes to the point of anarchy. But there was the ultimate ground for optimism. It was obvious that things could change for the better because they were in the course of doing so. People who had been unemployed were now working. People who had been forced to live in the US or the UK were coming home. Long-derelict sites were being filled, if not with fine buildings, then at least with something other than weeds and litter. Change wasn't just in the air – it was visible and tangible.

This was a tonic for a culture that had been steeped in fatalism. Some of the attractive sides of Irish life had been underpinned by that fatalism – the idea that things will probably be terrible in the long run, that there's nothing much we can do about it, and that we might as well have a good time while we're waiting. But, for a while, it seemed that the Irish could have a good time without expecting the worst to arrive eventually. There was an exuberance to Irish life, but one which seemed to be compatible with hard work and ambition. The strengths that had always been brought to bear by the Irish in exile – resourcefulness, adaptability, energy – seemed finally to have found their place at home.

It was easy to believe that the confidence and vigour of the new Ireland would have to find an outlet in political, moral and social change. It did not seem over-optimistic to imagine that this burgeoning society would quickly become impatient with a political system steeped in localism and mediocrity and patently unable to meet any of its own targets. Or that it would be sufficiently repelled by the continued existence of social squalor amid conspicuous affluence to demand at least a basic level of decency for all its citizens. Or that it would try to grasp the opportunity of having momentarily skipped to the front of post-industrial economics to reshape itself as a technologically literate and inventive culture.

What could scarcely be imagined amid all the tingling novelty, all the buzz and brassiness of the real Irish boom, was that there was a price to be paid for skipping modernity. It was a little too good to be true that Ireland could go from the pre-modern to the post-modern without ever fully creating the structures and habits of a modern democracy. Large chunks of classic democracy were missing – the shift from religious authority to public and civic morality; the idea that the state should operate objectively and impersonally rather than as a private network of mutual obligations; the notion of the law as a universal and neutral check on everyone's behaviour, whatever their status; the belief in an independent parliament that exists to legislate rather than to service clients and to make government accountable rather than to keep it in place at all costs.

In retrospect, plonking a hyper-charged globalised economy on top of such an underdeveloped system of political governance and public morality was always likely to create an unbearable strain. But only the most irredeemable pessimist would have predicted that the forces that would destroy the Celtic Tiger would be nineteenth-century revenants, come back to haunt its dreams of twenty-first-century success.

Yet, as this book has suggested, five of those forces combined to create the conditions in which the entire Celtic Tiger project foundered. A primitive, pre-modern land hunger created the new feudalism in which an elite puffed up the price of land and inflated a fatal property boom. The political system, embodied most thoroughly in Fianna Fáil, remained rooted in the Tammany Hall politics of the nineteenth-century Irish-American Democratic Party machines. Its interest in power and patronage to the virtual exclusion of all else meant that politics, when they needed to be imbued with ideas and ambition, were still defined by what 'one of the most senior figures in [Bertie] Ahern's administration' told the political journalist Pat Leahy: 'Politics is keeping enough people happy at the right time and taking the shit for the rest of the time.' A system of patronage and personal connection continued to operate, from the constituent being 'looked after' by the TD to the donor being 'looked after' by the minister.

In business, and especially in banking, there remained an anarchic attitude to law and morality, rooted both in a colonial habit of playing games with authority and in a religious culture that saw sex, rather than money, as the currency of sin. The bourgeoisie continued with its nineteenth-century attitude of valuing the professions above all, and certainly above science, maths and technology. And the heroic powers of denial, the ability to know and not know at the same time, that had been formed by the peculiar circumstances of Irish history, remained remarkably intact. Together these five forces created a crazed property boom, a reckless banking system, a lack of interest in the technologies that had created the boom, and a political and public mentality in which none of these realities could be grasped.

A rather peculiar conclusion follows from these truths. It is that in order to have a future, Ireland must complete the unfinished business of its past. It cannot go backwards, of course, and it will have to function in a globalised economy and the political context of the European Union. But it has to undertake some quite old-fashioned exercises in nation building. It has to recognise that, as an isolated backwater, it missed out on the big things that happened in other Western European states after the Second World War: the construction of the welfare state and the re-establishment of a modern democracy from scratch. Almost a century after the Irish Republic was notionally declared in 1916, it needs to found a Second Republic with the same conscious determination to rebuild from disaster that most of its European neighbours had to acquire after the cataclysm of the 1940s.

One certainty is that the impetus to do this will not come from the current establishment. In Iceland, the collapse of the banking system and the ruination of the economy led to sustained mass protests outside parliament and the central bank. The government was forced out of office and a new one with radically different policies was elected. In Ireland, which differed from Iceland only in having membership of the euro and the consequent support of the European Central Bank, there has been no sign that the political system has this capacity to renew itself. Neither from the outside (in terms of mass protests) nor from the inside has there been any coherent reaction at all.

The Irish establishment has been both remarkably (and shamelessly) resilient and fiercely determined to insist that no fundamental change has happened. The collapse of the Celtic Tiger is to be understood as a misfortune made a little worse by some minor misjudgements and bad timing. Bertie Ahern told the *Sunday Independent* in September 2009 that 'All of the time that we were dealing with the property issue, Charlie McCreevy and myself thought it was manageable to bring it, from the high, down to the medium, without it being a disaster. But what happened was the financial crisis came in and the world trade collapsed. All those external shocks coming together made it impossible to manage the position.' As for the abysmal lack of regulation, that was the fault of the regulators for not asking the government to bring in tougher laws: 'The Central Bank and the Financial Regulator seemed happy. They were never in to us saying "Listen, we must put legislation and control on the banks." That never happened.' Behind this self-serving waffle, there was a steely determination to ensure that the citizens would pay for the wild spree of the bankers and developers. The collapse of the banking system has left behind a terrible legacy of debt. With its decision in September 2008 to underwrite the entire system with blanket guarantees, the government began a classic process of throwing good money after bad. It ended up proposing to take development loans of €77 billion under the wing of the state's 'bad bank', the National Asset Management Agency (Nama), ensuring that the taxpayer would be saddled with the consequences of the property mania of the boom years.

Thus, instead of letting Anglo Irish Bank die, Fianna Fáil remained obsessed with saving it. To let Seánie FitzPatrick's monster slink off to a well-deserved demise would have been to admit that most of what had happened since 2002 was a dangerous delusion. It was necessary, therefore, to keep the zombie bank alive with abundant transfusions of public cash. Anglo Irish got €3.8 billion from the state when it was nationalised. It then formed the largest single part of the Nama operation – €28 billion of the €77 billion in loans that were to be assumed by the state. (With a discount of around 30 per cent on the loans, this meant that the taxpayer was essentially putting up around €20 billion to keep Anglo Irish afloat.) And even after this, it was reckoned that Anglo Irish would need something between €6 billion and €10 billion of public funds to keep it solvent.

Altogether, this meant that the government was putting, directly or indirectly, at least €30 billion into a bank with an appalling history of cooking its books, manipulating its share price and giving vast, secret loans to its own directors and executives. To put this sum in perspective, it is about the same as the expected total tax revenues of the Irish state in 2009.

The rationale for this subsidy was twofold. There was a belief that the Irish property market would somehow recover over the next decade and that Anglo's steaming midden of junk loans would therefore blossom with golden fruit for the taxpayer. And there was a dogged faith that a systemically corrupt bank that had never had much to do with the real economy of viable and sustainable businesses could somehow be transformed into a sensible, productive and economically useful institution. Just over the horizon there was a new world in which 'Anglo Irish Bank' would be a trusted international brand, 'regulated by the Irish Financial Regulator' would be a reassurance rather than a warning, and negative equity would be a bad memory.

The persistence of this mindset was surely the final proof that Fianna Fáil was incapable either of understanding what had happened or of radically reforming itself. The shock of the collapse had been profound, but it had not been deep enough to generate the conviction in government, in the higher levels of the civil service, in much of the media, or in large parts of the financial and business elites, that Ireland could not survive without radical change. The overwhelming feeling was that everything must be done – including pumping billions into an amoral and incompetent banking system and cutting social services like health and education – to ensure that nothing really changed. The impulse was to shore up the system, batten down the hatches and wait for deliverance by a global economic upturn.

No one in Fianna Fáil managed to express a coherent apology for bringing the country to its knees. The best the Taoiseach and former Minister for Finance Brian Cowen could manage in September 2009, a year after the disaster struck, was that 'if people want me to apologise, I apologise in the event that people think I did something purposely wrong'. One of Ireland's most successful businessmen, Niall Fitzgerald, a former chief executive of Unilever and a non-executive director of Bank of Ireland in the 1990s, recounted a dinner conversation with friends who still hold positions on the boards of Irish banks: 'I told them: "You have to make a choice. Did you not know what was going on? If you didn't, you must ask yourself, are you a competent director? And if you did know, you were complicit in recklessness and fraud. So which is it? Because there isn't anything in between."' The conversation, Fitzgerald recalled, was 'uncomfortable'. There was certainly no evidence that those in the business elite who served on the boards of banks were left with any sense of shame.

Given this inability of those in positions of power to come to terms with their responsibilities, there is little option but to look for a radical departure. Yet, as has already been suggested, this radicalism may consist of a return to a past that never was. The unfinished business of democratic modernity has to be the basis for an Irish recovery. There is a need to re-found the Republic. Such an act of re-foundation would have three cornerstones.

The first is the most abstract but also the most critical. There has to be a general recognition that the crisis is moral as well as economic. It is, indeed, a perfect illustration of the economics of morality – the absence of a sense of propriety, of restraint and of right and wrong, was not just obnoxious, it was economically disastrous. Public morality in this sense is all about sustainability. And sustainability is about knowing when to stop. Nothing in Ireland told people when to stop. The voters didn't set limits on the behaviour of politicians. Neither the politicians, nor any effective system of environmental protection and planning, set limits for the developers. The regulators didn't set limits for the banks. Unless there is an attitudinal revolution in which honesty, responsibility and a concern for the future become basic social values, nothing else is going to change. An end to the culture of impunity would certainly help, but that in turn would demand an end to the culture of denial and evasion. Irish people have to take hold of their own reality.

If they can do so, the second keystone of renewal can be put in place. This is a sweeping reform of the institutions of government. The elements of such a reform are obvious enough. There needs to be a proper system of local government, not just because it is a good thing in itself but because, in its absence, voters send politicians to the national parliament who really belong on local councils. This in turn would allow the Dáil to be slimmed down (in terms of numbers) and beefed up (in terms of power). A real functioning parliament that concentrates on the jobs of framing legislation and holding the executive to account may seem like a rather basic demand in an established democracy, but the reality is that Ireland has never had one.

Even this kind of institutional reform will be relatively useless, however, unless it is accompanied by a realignment of the political party system. The current alignment is still shaped by the two big, populist right-of-centre parties, Fianna Fáil and Fine Gael, whose origins go back to a civil war in 1923 and whose real differences have shrunk to virtual invisibility. Every possible alternative has to express itself as a marginal variation within the tribal power plays of what might be called Fianna Gael. The result is to produce a Henry Fordist politics in which voters can choose any government they like so long as it is essentially right of centre. This has made it almost impossible for the system to offer clear alternatives to voters. It has also sustained the habit of groupthink in which orthodoxies function as self-evident truths until they turn out to be fatal delusions.

The third element of a Second Republic is the articulation

of a social vision. The scale of Ireland's economic collapse, and the decision of the government to throw the remaining public resources at failed banks, means that a decade of relative hardship is all but inevitable. The immediate prospect for the country is a series of deflationary budgets, spiralling unemployment, a wave of mortgage defaults and savage cutbacks in already inadequate social services. This will probably lead to social unrest, but it will almost certainly lead to the return of a familiar mechanism: emigration.

If other Western economies begin to pick up while Ireland slogs through a long depression, the young and mobile will do what their ancestors did for hundreds of years. They will go. And this will throw Ireland back into a vortex from which it seemed to have escaped once and for all. Ireland was underdeveloped for so long because it was trapped in a vicious circle. Underdevelopment led to emigration which stripped out both population and the forces of change, reinforcing underdevelopment. In the mid-1990s, this vicious circle turned into a virtuous one: a rising economy attracted back emigrants, who in turn boosted the economy. If this process is reversed, Ireland could be facing much more than a decade of austerity.

To avoid this danger, Ireland needs to be able to offer its people more than a grim merry-go-round of deflationary budgets depressing the economy, leading to more deflationary budgets. The country has to invent a future for itself. It has to be able to articulate a concrete sense of what kind of place it wants to be. To do this, it has to engage with a wider reality: the era of the kind of free-market globalisation for which the Celtic Tiger became the poster child is over. What will most probably replace it is a much more highly regulated, slower-growing and state-directed market system in which security and quality of life outweigh the dream of getting rich quick.

The good news for Ireland is that it has just learned a particularly painful lesson in the lack of a direct connection between rampant economic growth on the one hand and a decent society on the other. The failure of the Celtic Tiger project leaves the population with a bittersweet reflection: the availability of money did not in itself lead to a good health service, top-class infrastructure in areas like public transport and communications, an education system that could support pretensions to a place at the leading edge of science and technology, or an end to consistent poverty. This may be depressing, but it has a more hopeful corollary. Real social progress comes from a combination of resources and vision. For the last decade, Ireland had the resources without the vision. For the next, it might have fewer resources but it can generate the ambition, the values and the energy to use them well.

Values, in political terms, are priorities. A system which has been built on the avoidance of explicit choices has to be refashioned so that it can, not simply make those choices, but generate a real consensus around them. To do that, it has to start with a sense of justice. There has to be a common understanding that Ireland can no longer afford to indulge fantasies of abundant wealth. Politicians and mandarins have to start seeing themselves as public servants, and being paid accordingly. Bankers and business executives have to define their status by something other than the outward rewards of greed. The non-taxpaying aristocracy has to be sent, figuratively at least, to the guillotine. A fair and transparent tax system, that takes most from those who have most, can produce, not just more public resources, but a sense of shared responsibility.

It is, under these conditions, perfectly possible to create a society in which life for the majority is actually better and more secure than it was during the height of the boom. If resources in the health system are not split between subsidised private medicine and underdeveloped public facilities, the same money can go a lot further. A very good public pension system could be created from the amount of money currently spent on the state pension plus the €3 billion annual subsidies to private pensions. The extravagant wastefulness of the property boom, in which huge resources were squandered on the creation of houses, hotels and offices that no one really wanted, can be turned to the provision of decent homes for everyone. Even in straitened times, a political system which gives priority to the meeting of basic needs (health, education, childcare, housing, pensions) and cuts out the swaggering, the pet projects and the pampering of an elite, can deliver real improvements for the majority of citizens. That in turn can replace the boomtime delusions of grandeur with a real sense of pride.

It is worth remembering, too, that in Ireland, as in all other developed societies, there was, beyond a certain point, no real relationship between money and happiness. Surveys showed that while GDP was doubling, the proportion of people declaring themselves 'very happy with the life you lead' actually declined steadily from a peak in 1997. This does not mean that there should be nostalgia for mass unemployment, emigration and poverty. But it does suggest that there is, for the Irish as for most human beings, a point at which basic needs are satisfied, a reasonable degree of security has been achieved and powerful but intangible feelings like belonging to a society in which one can feel some pride become possible.

That point is contained in one word that the Celtic Tiger did not have in its lexicon: 'enough'. Ireland cannot, and should not, seek to return to the hysterical hyper-capitalist growth of the period between 2002 and 2008. But if it keeps its eyes fixed on that point where enough is enough, it can, not just survive, but thrive. Its people have enough energy, enough talent, enough resourcefulness, enough imagination. The question is whether they have enough constructive anger to kick away a system that has failed them and make a new one for themselves.

Namaland

Before 2010 is out, the Irish people will be the proud possessors of some of the finest hotels in the world.

The art deco elegance and £35 afternoon teas of Claridge's? The neo-Edwardian grandeur and £8000-a-night
suites of the Connaught? The Lutyens blue walls and debu-
tante chic of the Berkeley? Ours, all ours. Along with about
200 other hotels and resorts, including, in Ireland, the Shelbourne, the K Club and the Ritz-Carlton.

It will, no doubt, be a comfort to those who have lost
their jobs or found themselves paying long-term mortgages
for houses that will never be worth what they've paid for
them, to picture such luxury. The property analyst Ronan
Lyons estimated that 40 per cent of homes in Ireland – or
340,000 houses – were worth less in 2009 than had been
paid for them. Another analysis – by the Economic and
Social Research Institute – suggested that those who bought
apartments in Dublin at the height of the boom in 2007 will
be in negative equity until 2030. Lyons also estimated in
February 2010 that more than half of all jobs for young men
under twenty-five had disappeared. How nice for those
inclined to whinge about such things to know, however, that
there was a good chance that Madonna or the Duchess of
Devonshire, Leonardo DiCaprio or the Sultan of Brunei,

might be soaking in their bathtub or sipping vintage champagne in their David Collins-designed bar.

Hotels like Claridge's and the Shelbourne are a legacy to the Irish people of property magnates like Derek Quinlan and Bernard McNamara. Quinlan, whose Maybourne group bought the London trophy hotels in 2004, quietly emigrated to Switzerland in August 2009, leaving an estimated €2 billion in development loans to be taken over by the state's bad bank, the National Asset Management Agency (Nama). Bernard McNamara, who along with a consortium of investors pumped an astonishing €265 million (almost exactly €1 million per room) into the Shelbourne, declared himself 'broke' in January 2010 with debts of around €1.5 billion.

It is, perhaps, unfair to cite luxury hotels like Claridge's and the Connaught as typical of the vast property empire that was being dumped on the Irish public through Nama. They are indeed untypical – they may actually be worth some money when they're sold. This is not, unfortunately, true of much of the junk for which, the government decided, the state would pay €54 billion to the banks who had accepted it as collateral for vast loans.

The sheer extent of the detritus washed on shore after the sinking of the Celtic Tiger was hard to grasp. The best estimate of the number of vacant houses came from the Urban Institute at University College Dublin. In March 2010, it worked out that there were 345,116 vacant residential properties in the state (including 64,000 holiday homes). This is 17.5 per cent of all the homes in the Republic of Ireland. Outside of the greater Dublin area, 21 per cent of houses are unoccupied. One home in every five is an empty shell. And these figures can be expected to rise: 'In fact with the economic downturn it is increasingly likely that vacancy levels could increase.'

Making things even worse, however, is the fact that many of these spectral homes are concentrated in ghost estates. Defining a 'ghost estate' as one in which at least half of the houses are empty, Justin Gleeson and Rob Kitchin of the National University of Ireland, Maynooth, conservatively estimated that there are 621 of these haunted zones. Even worse is that, while the phenomenon reaches into every county in Ireland, it is most concentrated in those with the lowest populations: Leitrim, with a population of 29,000 people, has twenty-one ghost estates. These properties may be less than worthless. There is no prospect of selling them, but they will cost money to maintain or even to demolish. The people living in these estates, most of them paying the inflated mortgages of the boom's peak years, are stuck in houses they cannot sell, sometimes without basic facilities like pavements, lighting or green areas.

As well as empty and half-built houses, the legacy of the boom includes perhaps 200 zombie hotels. Fianna Fáil's ludicrous tax reliefs for hotel builders, and the willingness of builders to do almost anything to avoid tax, resulted in a rash of hotels for which there was no demand. The sole result, with supply so far exceeding demand, was to make almost the entire hotel sector uneconomic. In 2009, hotel rates in Ireland crashed faster than in any comparable economy and became the cheapest in western Europe. (The average price of a room fell from €101 in 2008 to €80 in 2009.) The Irish Hotels Federation reckoned that 15,000 rooms needed to be taken out of the system for the rest of the trade to become viable. Given that most of these rooms are in hotels built by developers with loans from the banks, it is probable that most of these useless assets will also end up in Nama. Again, many of these properties are worse than useless – they actually cost money to run, even at a loss.

When the public has got a glimpse – almost always through court cases – of the real value of other properties that it is about to own, the truth has been terrifying. Development lands in Athlone, valued at €31 million by Bank of Ireland in 2006, were worth €600,000 in February 2010. Lands at Sallins, County Kildare, valued at €17.5 million on the bank's books, were actually worth just €4 million. The infamous Irish Glass Bottle site in Dublin's docklands, purchased by McNamara and other investors (including the state-owned Dublin Docklands Development Authority) for €412 million in 2006, is now valued at €50 million. In 2009 alone, the average price paid for an acre of farmland dropped by 43 per cent. And agricultural land is what many of the large tracts rezoned for development, and thus theoretically rendered vastly more valuable, will revert to. In February 2010, Waterford county council published draft plans showing huge areas bought by developers at 'astronomical' prices reverting to farming. Other local authorities were sure to follow suit. The implications for Nama are as obvious as they are disastrous. At least a third and possibly more than half of Nama's portfolio is development land.

Yet Nama is based – at least for public consumption – on one basic calculation. Nama will pay €54 billion to the banks for property loans supposedly worth €47 billion. The gap will supposedly be filled by the 'long term economic value' of the properties. Put simply, in order for Nama to pay its way, even on the government's highly optimistic figures, Irish property prices will have to rise by 10 per cent over the next decade. This is not so much an assumption, more a necessary fantasy.

As we've seen, Nama's portfolio, alongside its trophy properties like Claridge's or Battersea power station (owned by the Nama-bound Treasury Holdings), contains a lot of stuff that is virtually worthless. The idea that any of the junk will ever be worth more than a tiny fraction of what was paid for it in boomtime Ireland is absurd. In the first place, there is a massive over-supply of buildings like houses and hotels. Even if Ireland were suddenly to return to prosperity and growth, the huge overhang of surplus development will depress prices for a very long time.

Secondly, a 10 per cent rise in property prices would mean taking them back to where they were in 2003 or 2004. But this would mean a return to the extraordinarily high levels of bank lending in the boom years. Underlying the property bubble was a massive expansion in credit. This was, up to a point, consistent with a more general credit bubble. In other Eurozone countries and the UK, bank lending to private individuals typically rose from 80 per cent of GDP to 100 per cent between 1997 and 2008. But in Ireland, it rose from 60 per cent to 200 per cent. And much of this was pumped into the property market. As Morgan Kelly pointed out, 'Irish banks were lending 40 per cent more in real terms to property developers alone in 2008 than they had been lending to everyone in Ireland in 2000, and 75 per cent more as mortgages.'

That wave of credit has slowed to a trickle. In 2006, Irish banks gave out almost €40 billion in mortgages. In 2009, the total was just over €8 billion. Given the collapse of the Irish banks, and the fact that they will emerge from the immediate crisis as far smaller entities, a return to anything like those levels of credit is impossible. Even if it were possible, however, it would be insane.

The reality is that, through Nama, the government is giving the banks €54 billion for assets that are certainly worth nothing like the claimed €47 billion and that are unlikely to increase significantly in value over the decade-long lifespan of the agency. Even if, by some extraordinary fluke, they were to do so, it could only be through the re-inflation of a property bubble that destroyed the Irish economy. For Nama to work, all government policy will have to be directed towards attempting to increase property prices. Essentially, Nama is the final expression of the mentality of the boom-time – having set up the property developer as the quintessential figure of contemporary Ireland, the country itself is now to become a nation of property developers.

Even before Nama was actually operating, the effects of this mentality were already apparent. In the real Irish economy, it was crucial that commercial rents be rapidly reduced so that retailers could stay in business. (The value of retail sales fell by 18 per cent in 2009, making it the worst year in living memory.) Large numbers of jobs were being lost. Almost unbelievably, however, landlords pushed up rents. Higher rents inflated the apparent worth of commercial properties destined for Nama. Thus, at Dundrum shopping centre in south Dublin – itself something of a symbol of the high tide of consumerism before the crash – the landlords, Castlethorn Construction, demanded a 60 per cent rent increase from traders in March 2010.

Given all of this, an obvious question arises: how did they get away with it? Nama was controversial among economists (both those on the right who actually believe in capitalism and those on the left who believe in social justice) and polls showed that a large majority of the public either opposed it or was too baffled by it to have an opinion. In an

Irish Times poll in September 2009, Nama got the support of just 26 per cent of respondents. A similar poll showed just 32 per cent believing that Nama is the right approach. But, after a carefully managed fit of conscience in the Green Party, it sailed through the parliamentary process almost entirely unscathed. A breathtaking proposition – that the public should pay vastly over the odds for properties that the banks had lent testosterone-crazed speculative developers far too much money to buy – came to be accepted as an inevitable fact.

This was partly achieved through outright obfuscation. The money Nama is giving to the banks is borrowed by the state from the European Central Bank (ECB). (Though, in a continuation of the culture of fiscal cuisine, it is kept off the balance sheet of state debt by the transparent ruse of pretending that it is being borrowed by a private entity.) This money in turn is given to the banks in the form of bonds. The banks are supposed to use these bonds to allow them to lend money to customers, but as the government's own economic advisor Alan Ahearne admitted, they are free to simply trade them on financial markets. From this somewhat complicated structure, Fianna Fáil spun a grossly deceptive tale: that the billions being given to the banks don't represent Irish taxpayers' cash at all.

This outrageous fiction was put forward with a completely straight face by Fianna Fáil's spokesman, Frank Fahey. Fahey knows a thing or two about the property market. The register of interests shows that he has apartments, houses and commercial property in Castlerea, Galway, Athlone, Limerick, Gort, Dubai, Boston, Brussels, France, Portugal and Dublin. On this authority, he was able to pronounce in late 2009 that Nama will work because 'the property market will rebound . . . it has already started'. More importantly, however, he informed listeners to RTE radio that the money borrowed for Nama is 'not taxpayers' money. It is ECB money.' Arguing against Fine Gael's George Lee, he declared indignantly that 'I cannot believe, George, that you're saying that this [money] will come from the taxpayer. This money will be paid in government bonds which will then be cashed.' Either Fahey was stupid enough to believe that bonds are not real money or, more probably, Fianna Fáil believed that a significant part of the public would be stupid enough to believe it.

If the tabloid version of the Nama spin was that we were getting magic money from somewhere, there was a more sophisticated argument for the broadsheet readers. This was that, while the necessity of putting virtually all of Ireland's discretionary resources into the portfolios accumulated by crazed speculators was regrettable, it would have beneficial effects. In the long run, Nama would pay its way when the property market returned to buoyancy. In the short term, meanwhile, it would create conditions in which the Irish banks would start to lend money again and sweet streams of credit would flow into the parched desert of the Irish economy. Or to put it another way, without Nama, Ireland would be left with zombie banks. As the Finance Minister Brian Lenihan expressed it, 'Nama will ensure that we avoid the Japanese outcome of "zombie banks" that are just ticking over and not making a vibrant contribution to economic growth.'

There were two glaring problems with this argument. There is absolutely no obligation on the banks to use the money they get from offloading their junk loans to extend credit to Irish businesses. On the contrary, they are far more likely to use the bulk of it to put a gloss of respectability on their ravaged balance sheets. And in any case, more than half of the Nama funds are going to what are already zombie banks. Anglo Irish couldn't be more obviously zombie if it was renamed the Hiberno-Haitian Bank. And it never mattered to the real economy in the first place. It was systemically important to the Irish economy in the way that the Huns were systemically important to the Roman Empire.

Of the €77 billion in loans that Nama is to take on, around €40 billion is held by Anglo Irish and its junior wannabe Irish Nationwide Building Society. In justifying Nama and cash injections to these institutions, Lenihan consistenly claimed that they were of 'systemic importance' to the Irish economy. This is simply absurd. Just 11 per cent of Anglo's loan book is categorised as 'business banking'. Almost all of the rest relates to the property and construction sectors – that is, to the bubble economy that was parasitic on the real one. Irish Nationwide, as a mutual building society, was supposed to be in the business of giving mortgages to people to buy houses. In fact, just 22 per cent of its loan book relates to residential property. In September 2008, the last month before the crisis hit and the government guaranteed its deposits, Irish Nationwide approved precisely zero home loans for first-time buyers. Its real business was mainlining money into the veins of addicted and delusional developers.

However, Irish Nationwide's boss, Michael 'Fingers' Fingleton, like Anglo's Sean Fitzpatrick, was well connected. RTE revealed, for example, that Fingleton (who left Nationwide with a pension of €27 million) had personally fast-tracked a loan of €1.6 million to Charlie McCreevy to buy a property at the plush K Club golf resort which was worth just €1.5

million – breaching guidelines that prohibited 100 per cent mortgages. Other Fianna Fáil figures who received help from Fingleton included Bertie Ahern's partner Celia Larkin. Larkin got a fast-tracked loan of €40,000 from Fingleton in March 2008, when Ahern was still Taoiseach, without the usual trivialities of showing proof of her income, identification, current account statements or details of other loans she had drawn down. The loan was politically important. It related to a transaction being investigated by the Mahon tribunal in which €30,000 apparently in a Fianna Fáil account was used to buy a house for Larkin's aunt. Ahern insisted that this money was a loan – hence the importance of it being repayed with interest by Larkin while the tribunal was sitting. There was nothing illegal about Fingleton's helpfulness in this instance but it did show the extent of the personal connections between Nationwide and those around Ahern. While the objective case for saving either Anglo or Nationwide with public money was weak, the emotional attachment of Fianna Fáil to Seanie and Fingers weighed heavily on the other side of the argument.

The only other argument for Nama was the vague generalisation that Ireland simply could not afford to let a bank go under. Lenihan explained to the Dáil in January 2009 that 'as a country, we cannot afford to have the message going out that we will let a bank fail'. In June 2009, when he was extending the bank guarantee, he repeated the message: 'The fundamental question that arises in connection with the guarantee concerns the fact that the Government decided it could not let a bank fail.'

This sounded like a point of absolute principle and thus like some sort of axiom from which a rational response could follow. But it, too, was nonsense. In February 2010, it was announced, to large-scale political indifference, that Post-bank, jointly owned by the Irish post office, An Post, and BNP Paribas, would be wound down by the end of the year. Brian Lenihan's reaction to its closure was a metaphorical yawn. He managed only to suggest that he was 'disappoint-ed [that word again] but not surprised'.

Postbank was a new, small, but growing provider of finan-cial services to ordinary people and local businesses. It had deposits of €450 million and 170,000 customers. It had 70,000 savings and 35,000 current accounts, 90,000 insur-ance policy holders and 10,000 credit-card customers. It did what banks used to do – provide financial services for people in their own communities. Because it operated through a thousand post offices, it was particularly important in towns, villages and working-class urban areas that have long since been abandoned by the main banks. More importantly, in any sane approach to the banking collapse, Postbank would have been an important part of a new strategy of creating sensible, community-based banks for individuals and small businesses.

But none of this is of systemic importance to the economy. To achieve that enviable status and become immortal, Post-bank would have had to do certain things. It would have needed a chief executive who was on first-name terms with the Taoiseach and who delivered regular lectures to the nation on the evils of social welfare and regulation. It would have had to plead with every gambler and hustler to please, please take a few hundred million more in loans for another fantasy project. It would have had to bamboozle its investors by cooking the books and lending chosen customers the money to buy its own shares. If it had concentrated on these goals instead of getting stuck in the pathetically old-fashioned rut of helping ordinary people manage money, it would have been systemically important.

So, Nama was based on four patently false propositions: that the €57 billion it will cost is not taxpayers' money; that property values are almost certain to rise substantially over the next decade; that this vast subsidy will result in the availability of ample credit for the real economy; and that the Irish state does not let banks fail.

Underlying these propositions was a barely conscious but powerful assumption: that Ireland was rich enough to absorb all the follies of the boom-time property mania. There was a weird but fundamental contradiction in the official mindset. On the one hand, Ireland was held (rightly) to be in the midst of an existential economic crisis in which its apparent wealth had evaporated. On the other, the Irish state was held to be in a position to pay €57 billion (almost twice its newly shrunken annual tax take) into Nama as well as putting perhaps €15 to €20 billion in straight cash into the banks. This was another, spectacular example of the unknown known. One half of the official brain knew that Ireland was broke. Another was embarking on the most astonishing spending spree in the history of the state.

The underlying truth was not only that Ireland was emphatically not rich in 2010 but that it had never really been so. For all the talk of becoming one of the richest nations in the world, Ireland, even in terms of per capita income, was a middle-ranking eurozone country: eighth of sixteen eurozone countries in 2009 and set to fall sharply in 2010 as the economy contracted further. But income is not wealth. Rossa White of Davy Research pointed out in early 2010 that 'Estimates of the capital stock show Ireland lagging behind. Irish residents would hardly claim that this country is wealthier than other small euro-area countries such as Finland or Belgium. Infrastructure – roads, rail, schools, hospitals and telecommunications – is far superior in those nations.' The problem is that, as with so much else, the apparently rapid growth in capital stock in the boom years was largely delusional. Ostensibly, capital stock soared by 157 per cent between 2000 and 2008. But in reality, two thirds of this was accounted for by the housing bubble. Private sector productive capital stock increased by a paltry 26 per cent in those eight years. So much of the income boom had been squandered on property and consumption that what was left over in terms of tangible infrastructure was still much poorer than in comparable countries.

And of course, Ireland was in hock to an almost unfathomable extent. By the end of January 2010, according to the Central Bank, Irish residents (individuals, companies and corporations) had amassed almost €1.1 trillion in debt. Most of this – €789 billion – was accounted for by companies in the Irish Financial Services Centre, but that still left nearly €200 billion in debt securities owed by Irish banks, long-term government debt of €78 billion and outstanding residential mortgages of almost €150 billion.

The paradox, then, was that Ireland needed a fiscal stimulus of serious infrastructural investment more than its neighbours and trading partners. But with all the available resources going in to the banks, it was getting savage cutbacks instead. Fianna Fáil, which had boasted through Charlie McCreevy of the ultimate anti-Keynesian gesture of spending money when it had it and not spending it when it didn't, was continuing with its pro-cyclical approach. It had hyper-inflated the economy by stimulating an economy that was already doing a decent impression of a gaggle of five-year-olds let loose in a Coca Cola factory. Now it was strangling a gasping economy by slashing public sector wages and social welfare payments and cutting spending, including infrastructural investment.

How, though, did it get away with taking money off unemployed people and those who cleaned ministerial offices to spend it on the worthless 'assets' of Anglo Irish Bank? Why did protestors in Greece end up chanting 'We are not Ireland!', meaning 'We are not passive stooges!'?

Why were the Irish so passive? Part of the answer undoubtedly lies in fear. The very scale of the mortgage debts that so many people had been left with created a sense of terror, especially in a climate of high job losses and deep insecurity. Part of the answer lies, too, in a successful campaign to create a new enemy – public sector workers.

Initially, when the crisis began to unfold, anger was directed at bankers, developers and at Fianna Fáil itself. The idea that public sector workers were to blame was obviously absurd. The government's chief economic advisor, Alan Ahearne, made this clear in the *Irish Times* in January 2009: 'I suspect that much of the rhetoric in the media about public sector pay and reform is an attempt by some of the least well-informed commentators to distract attention from the main source of our economic woes. The mess in which the Irish economy finds itself largely stems from the house price bubble, not from problems in the public sector. It is probably not a coincidence that some of the most vocal critics of the public sector today were among the most conspicuous cheerleaders for the housing boom.'

Ahearne also pointed out that while cuts in public sector pay were in his view necessary, their effect would be relatively marginal: 'an often overlooked point is that even large-

scale public sector pay cuts would only have a moderate
effect on the fiscal deficit. A 10 per cent reduction in public
sector pay and pensions, for example, would reduce government spending by €2 billion. But when account is taken of
the associated loss of tax revenues (both direct and indirect),
the net reduction in the budget deficit would be a little more
than €1 billion.'

Yet, however limited its real usefulness, attacking the public sector and cutting the wages of civil and public servants
paid very high political dividends. It fed in to a deep anger at
the failure of the state and its institutions, but channelled
that anger against those who provided state services rather
than those who corrupted politics and abased the state
before the interests of a small minority. What Ahearne had
rightly seen as a problem – 'distract[ing] attention from the
main source of our economic woes' – was, for his employers,
a blessing.

Fear and distraction played their part, then. But beneath
these emotions and strategies, there was something much
deeper – a sense of impotence. As with so much else in Irish
public culture, there was a vicious circle. The political system
failed catastrophically, in part because of the absence of
coherent public engagement. But that failure in turn suggested that public engagement was futile. The more incompetent
and feckless the system of government, the more people
turned away from the public realm in disgust and despair.
Short-term political insurgencies, like the election to the Dáil
of the popular RTE economics correspondent George Lee on
a wave of hope and anger, proved illusory, as Lee resigned
after just nine months.

Yet the crisis is too profound – and will probably be too
long-lasting – for disengagement and disillusion to be sus-

tainable options. The solutions being offered by the government will not work and may, indeed, make the crisis deeper. Sooner or later, the Irish people themselves will have to re-invent politics, civic morality and the public realm. No one else is going to do that for them.

Index

ff

Faber and Faber – a home for writers

Faber and Faber is one of the great independent publishing houses in London. We were established in 1929 by Geoffrey Faber and our first editor was T. S. Eliot. We are proud to publish prize-winning fiction and non-fiction, as well as an unrivalled list of modern poets and playwrights. Among our list of writers we have five Booker Prize winners and eleven Nobel Laureates, and we continue to seek out the most exciting and innovative writers at work today.

www.faber.co.uk – a home for readers

The Faber website is a place where you will find all the latest news on our writers and events. You can listen to podcasts, preview new books, read specially commissioned articles and access reading guides, as well as entering competitions and enjoying a whole range of offers and exclusives. You can also browse the list of Faber Finds, an exciting new project where reader recommendations are helping to bring a wealth of lost classics back into print using the latest on-demand technology.